revised edition

Connect

**Jack C. Richards
Carlos Barbisan**
com Chuck Sandy

Combo 1
Student's book

CAMBRIDGE UNIVERSITY PRESS

CAMBRIDGE
UNIVERSITY PRESS

University Printing House, Cambridge CB2 8BS, United Kingdom

One Liberty Plaza, 20th Floor, New York, NY 10006, USA

477 Williamstown Road, Port Melbourne, VIC 3207, Australia

314–321, 3rd Floor, Plot 3, Splendor Forum, Jasola District Centre, New Delhi – 110025, India

103 Penang Road, #05-06/07, Visioncrest Commercial, Singapore 238467

Cambridge University Press is part of the University of Cambridge.

It furthers the University's mission by disseminating knowledge in the pursuit of education, learning and research at the highest international levels of excellence.

www.cambridge.org

© Cambridge University Press 2015

This publication is in copyright. Subject to statutory exception
and to the provisions of relevant collective licensing agreements,
no reproduction of any part may take place without the written
permission of Cambridge University Press.

First published 2004
Second edition 2009
Revised edition 2015

20 19 18 17 16 15 14 13 12 11

Printed in Brazil by Forma Certa Grafica Digital LTDA

A catalogue record for this publication is available from the British Library

ISBN 978-1-107-53994-5 Combo 1

Additional resources for this publication at www.cambridge.org.br/connectarcade

Cambridge University Press has no responsibility for the persistence or accuracy of URLs for external or third-party internet websites referred to in this publication, and does not guarantee that any content on such websites is, or will remain, accurate or appropriate. Information regarding prices, travel timetables, and other factual information given in this work is correct at the time of first printing but Cambridge University Press does not guarantee the accuracy of such information thereafter.

Table of Contents

Syllabus iv

Unit 1 Back to School
Lesson 1 Classmates 2
Lesson 2 Hello. 4
Mini-review 6
Lesson 3 After school. 8
Lesson 4 Names 10
Get Connected 12
Review 14

Unit 2 Favorite People
Lesson 5 Teachers and friends 16
Lesson 6 Favorite stars. 18
Mini-review 20
Lesson 7 Birthdays. 22
Lesson 8 E-pals 24
Get Connected 26
Review 28

Unit 3 Everyday Things
Lesson 9 What a mess! 30
Lesson 10 Cool things 32
Mini-review 34
Lesson 11 Favorite things 36
Lesson 12 Where is it? 38
Get Connected 40
Review 42

Unit 4 Around Town
Lesson 13 At the movies 44
Lesson 14 Downtown 46
Mini-review 48
Lesson 15 At the mall 50
Lesson 16 Any suggestions? 52
Get Connected 54
Review 56

Unit 5 Family and Home
Lesson 17 My family 58
Lesson 18 Family reunion 60
Mini-review 62
Lesson 19 My new city 64
Lesson 20 At home 66
Get Connected 68
Review 70

Unit 6 At School
Lesson 21 The media center 72
Lesson 22 Around school 74
Mini-review 76
Lesson 23 School subjects. 78
Lesson 24 Spring Day 80
Get Connected 82
Review 84

Unit 7 Around the World
Lesson 25 People and countries 86
Lesson 26 Nationalities 88
Mini-review 90
Lesson 27 Holidays 92
Lesson 28 Important days 94
Get Connected 96
Review 98

Unit 8 Teen Time
Lesson 29 Favorite places 100
Lesson 30 Talent show 102
Mini-review 104
Lesson 31 School fashion 106
Lesson 32 Teen tastes 108
Get Connected 110
Review 112

Games 114

Get Connected Vocabulary Practice ... 122

Theme Projects 126

Word List 134

Unit 1 — Back to School

Lesson	Function	Grammar	Vocabulary
Lesson 1 Classmates	Introducing yourself	What's your name?	Ways to say hello
Lesson 2 Hello.	Greeting someone	How are you?	Greetings
Lesson 3 After school	Introducing others	this is (name)	Ways to say good-bye
Lesson 4 Names	Spelling names	Names	Common American names
Get Connected	Reading • Listening • Writing		
Theme Project	Make a personal information poster.		

Unit 2 — Favorite People

Lesson	Function	Grammar	Vocabulary
Lesson 5 Teachers and friends	Talking about teachers and friends	his / her Who's this?	Teachers and classmates
Lesson 6 Favorite stars	Talking about favorite stars	He's / She's . . .	Stars and their jobs
Lesson 7 Birthdays	Talking about age	How old . . . ? He's not / She's not	Numbers 0–20
Lesson 8 E-pals	Talking about where someone is from	Where . . . from? You're / I'm not	Countries
Get Connected	Reading • Listening • Writing		
Theme Project	Make a poster about two people who work at your school.		

Unit 3 — Everyday Things

Lesson	Function	Grammar	Vocabulary
Lesson 9 What a mess!	Describing who owns specific things	This is / That's + possessive	Things students own
Lesson 10 Cool things	Talking about interesting things	What's this / that?	Interesting objects
Lesson 11 Favorite things	Talking about favorite things	What are these / those?	Things students collect
Lesson 12 Where is it?	Talking about where things are located	Where's / Where are . . . ? It's not / They're not . . .	Objects in a bedroom
Get Connected	Reading • Listening • Writing		
Theme Project	Make an advertisement for an electronics store.		

Unit 4 — Around Town

Lesson	Function	Grammar	Vocabulary
Lesson 13 At the movies	Asking where someone is	Are you . . . ?	Places in town
Lesson 14 Downtown	Describing where something is	Is it . . . ?	More places in town Locations
Lesson 15 At the mall	Talking about where people are	Is she / Are they . . . ?	Places in the mall
Lesson 16 Any suggestions?	Making suggestions	Suggestions for others Suggestions for you + others	At the beach
Get Connected	Reading • Listening • Writing		
Theme Project	Make a guide for visitors to your city.		

Unit 5 **Family and Home**	Lesson	Function	Grammar	Vocabulary
	Lesson 17 My family	Talking about family members	have / has	Numbers 21–100 Family members
	Lesson 18 Family reunion	Describing what someone is like	What's . . . like?	Appearance and personality traits
	Lesson 19 My new city	Describing new neighborhoods and friends	We're / They're; Our / Their	Adjectives to describe places and people
	Lesson 20 At home	Describing a home	It has . . .	Areas of a house
	Get Connected	Reading • Listening • Writing		
	Theme Project	Make a group photo album.		

Unit 6 **At School**	Lesson	Function	Grammar	Vocabulary
	Lesson 21 The media center	Talking about what is in a room	There's / There are . . . There's no / There are no . . .	Things in a media center
	Lesson 22 Around school	Asking about school facilities	Is there a / Are there any . . . ?	School facilities
	Lesson 23 School subjects	Describing a class schedule	on / at	School subjects Saying the time
	Lesson 24 Spring Day	Talking about time and when events begin	What time . . . ?	Special events
	Get Connected	Reading • Listening • Writing		
	Theme Project	Make a poster of a dream school ("cool school").		

Unit 7 **Around the World**	Lesson	Function	Grammar	Vocabulary
	Lesson 25 People and countries	Talking about where people are from	is / isn't; are / aren't in short answers	Countries
	Lesson 26 Nationalities	Describing famous people	isn't / aren't in statements	Nationalities
	Lesson 27 Holidays	Talking about holidays	When is . . . ?	Months of the year Holidays
	Lesson 28 Important days	Describing favorite months	in / on	Dates and ordinal numbers
	Get Connected	Reading • Listening • Writing		
	Theme Project	Make an informational booklet about different countries.		

Unit 8 **Teen Time**	Lesson	Function	Grammar	Vocabulary
	Lesson 29 Favorite places	Talking about favorite places	What's it like?	Adjectives to describe places
	Lesson 30 Talent show	Describing talents	can / can't	Talents
	Lesson 31 School fashion	Talking about school uniforms	What color is / are . . . ?	Clothing Colors
	Lesson 32 Teen tastes	Talking about likes and dislikes	love / like / don't like	Music Food
	Get Connected	Reading • Listening • Writing		
	Theme Project	Make a pair of bookmarks of healthy foods and activities.		

Lesson 1

Classmates

1. Saying hello

🎧 **A** It is the first day of school at Kent International School. Listen and practice.
T.2

> Hi. I'm Nicole.

> Hello. I'm Yoshi.

> Hello. My name is Sandra.

> Hi. I'm Jenny.

> Hi. My name is Paulo.

> Hello. I'm Tyler.

🎧 **B** Listen again. Write the names.
T.3

1. *Paulo*
2. _____
3. _____
4. _____
5. _____
6. _____

UNIT 1 Back to School

2

2. Language focus

A Jenny and Paulo meet. Listen and practice.

Jenny Hi. I'm Jenny.
What's your name?
Paulo My name is Paulo.
Jenny Nice to meet you, Paulo.
Paulo Nice to meet you, too.

> **What's your name?**
>
> **What's your name?**
> **My name is** Paulo.
> **I'm** Jenny.
>
> What's = What is   I'm = I am

B Complete the conversations. Listen and check. Then practice.

1. **Jenny** What's __your__ (you / your) name?
   Sandra _____ (My / Your) name is Sandra.

2. **Yoshi** Hello. _____ (I'm / You) Yoshi.
   Paulo Nice to meet _____ (you / your), Yoshi.

3. **Nicole** I'm Nicole. _____ (Is / What's) your name?
   Tyler _____ (My / You) name is Tyler.

4. **Sandra** Hi. My _____ (nice / name) is Sandra.
   Yoshi _____ (My / I'm) Yoshi. Nice to meet you.

3. Speaking

Introduce yourself to three classmates.

You Hello. I'm .... What's your name?
Classmate My name is ....
You Nice to meet you, ...
Classmate Nice to meet you, too.

Back to School 3

Lesson 2: Hello.

1. Greetings

🎧 **Samantha greets people. Listen and practice.**
T.6

1
Good morning, Samantha.
Sorry I'm late, Mr. White.

2
Good afternoon, Mrs. Morgan.
Hello, Samantha.

3
Good evening, Miss Clark.
Hi, Samantha.

Titles		Single	Married
Females	Miss	✓	☐
	Mrs.	☐	✓
	Ms.	✓	✓
Males	Mr.	✓	✓

2. Listening

🎧 **Which greetings do you hear? Listen and check (✓) two greetings for each conversation.**
T.7

	Good morning.	Good afternoon.	Good evening.	Hi.	Hello.
Conversation 1	☐	✓	☐	☐	✓
Conversation 2	☐	☐	☐	☐	☐
Conversation 3	☐	☐	☐	☐	☐
Conversation 4	☐	☐	☐	☐	☐

Unit 1

3. Language focus

A Ms. Davis and Sandra greet each other. Listen and practice.

Ms. Davis Good morning, Sandra. How are you today?
Sandra Fine, thank you. How about you?
Ms. Davis Great, thanks. Are you ready for the new school year?
Sandra Yes, I am.

B Study the language chart.

How are you?		
How are you?		
Great.	Fine. Good. OK. Not bad.	Not too good.
😊	🙂	🙁

C Complete the conversations with the words in the boxes. Listen and check. Then practice.

☑ are ☐ not ☐ too ☐ you

1. Tyler Good morning. How __are__ you?
   Sandra _____ bad, thanks. How about _____ ?
   Tyler Not _____ good.

☐ afternoon ☐ good ☐ how ☐ you

2. Ms. Davis Good _____ , Paulo. How are you today?
   Paulo OK. _____ about you?
   Ms. Davis _____ , thank _____ .

4. Speaking

Greet three classmates.

Good....... How are you?

.... How about you?

Back to School 5

Lessons 1 & 2 Mini-review

1. Language check

A Complete the chart with words in the box. Use two words twice.

☐ Miss ☐ Mrs. ☐ Mr. ☐ Ms.

	Single	Married
Females	Miss	_____
	_____	_____
Males	_____	_____

B Number the sentences in the correct order.

1. ____ Nice to meet you, Tina.
   _1_ Hi. I'm Marco. What's your name?
   ____ My name is Tina.
   ____ Nice to meet you, too.

2. ____ Fine, thanks.
   ____ Yes, I am.
   ____ Good morning, Ms. Moss. How are you?
   ____ OK, thank you. How about you?
   ____ Are you ready for the new school year?

3. ____ Not bad.
   ____ OK, thanks. How are you?
   ____ Yes, I am.
   ____ Are you ready for class today?
   ____ Good afternoon, Mr. James. Sorry I'm late. How are you?

4. ____ Nice to meet you, Josh.
   ____ Are you ready for the new school year?
   ____ Hello. My name is Jim.
   ____ Yes, I am.
   ____ Hi, Jim. I'm Josh.
   ____ Nice to meet you, too.

6   Unit 1

**C Complete the conversations with the sentences in the box.
Then practice.**

☐ Hi, Wendy.   ☐ Nice to meet you, Ethan.   ☑ What's your name?
☐ How are you?   ☐ Not bad.

First day of school

Wendy Hi. I'm Wendy. _What's your name?_
Ethan My name is Ethan.
Wendy _____

Second day of school

Ethan _____
Wendy Hello, Ethan. _____
Ethan Good, thanks. How about you?
Wendy _____

2. Listening

A What's next? Listen and check (✓) the correct response.
T.10

1. ☐ Great, thanks.
   ☑ I'm Joseph.

2. ☐ Thank you.
   ☐ Good morning.

3. ☐ Fine, thanks.
   ☐ My name is Jennifer.

4. ☐ Not too good.
   ☐ Nice to meet you.

5. ☐ Hello, Dan. Sorry I'm late.
   ☐ How about you?

6. ☐ Good evening, Elizabeth.
   ☐ Nice to meet you, too.

B Now listen to the complete conversations. Check your answers.
T.11

Time for a Game?
See page 114.

Back to School

Lesson 3 After school

1. Language focus

A Nicole joins the basketball team. Listen and practice.

T.12

> **this is (name)**
> Mr. Diaz, **this is** Nicole Martel.
> Nicole, **this is** Mr. Diaz.

Tyler Hi, Nicole. How are you?
Nicole Good, thanks.

Tyler Mr. Diaz, this is Nicole Martel.

Tyler Nicole, this is Mr. Diaz.
Nicole Hi, Mr. Diaz. Nice to meet you.
Mr. Diaz Nice to meet you, too.

Mr. Diaz OK. Are you ready? Let's go!

B Introduce two classmates to each other.

You ...., this is ....
......., this is ....
Classmate 1 Hi, ...
Classmate 2 Hi, ... Nice to meet you.

C Complete the conversations with the words in the box.
Which conversation is an introduction? Circle it.

☐ are   ☐ good   ☐ hello   ☑ is   ☐ you

1. **Jenny** Hi, Mr. Diaz. This __is__ Paulo Santos.
   Mr. Diaz Hello, Paulo.
   Paulo Nice to meet _____, Mr. Diaz.

2. **Tyler** _____, Sandra.
   Sandra Hi, Tyler. How _____ you?
   Tyler _____, thanks.

2. Listening

🎧 Are these conversations introductions?
T.13 Listen and check (✓) *Yes* or *No*.

	Yes	No		Yes	No
Conversation 1	✓	☐	Conversation 4	☐	☐
Conversation 2	☐	☐	Conversation 5	☐	☐
Conversation 3	☐	☐			

3. Saying good-bye

🎧 **A** Listen and practice.
T.14

Good night, Mr. Diaz.
Good-bye, Paulo.
Bye, Tyler.
See you later.
See you tomorrow.
Bye-bye, Nicole.

B Complete the conversations. Then practice with a partner.
Use your own information.

1. **A** Good-__bye__, Sue.   **B** _____ you later, Jack.
2. **A** _____ night, Mr. Lee.   **B** Bye-bye, Dave.
3. **A** Bye-bye, Kendra.   **B** See _____ tomorrow, Min!

Back to School

Lesson 4 Names

1. Vocabulary

A Listen to these common American names. Then practice.
T.15

Girls' names			Boys' names		
Annie	Kaitlyn	Olivia	David	Matthew	Tyler
Elizabeth	Madison	Samantha	Ethan	Michael	William
Emma	Mia	Sophia	Jack	Ryan	Zachary
Hannah			John		

B Listen to the alphabet. Then practice.
T.16

Aa Bb Cc Dd Ee Ff Gg Hh Ii Jj Kk Ll Mm
Nn Oo Pp Qq Rr Ss Tt Uu Vv Ww Xx Yy Zz

C How do these students spell their names?
T.17   Listen and write the names. Then practice.

1. _Alex_   2. _____   3. _____   4. _____   5. _____

2. Pronunciation Syllables

A Study the pronunciation chart. Then listen and practice.
T.18

1 syllable	2 syllables	3 syllables
John	An nie	Za cha ry

B Listen to these names. How many syllables do they have?
T.19

1. Samantha _3_   2. Jack ____   3. Ethan ____   4. Madison ____   5. David ____

10   Unit 1

3. Language focus

A Adriana gets a library card.
Listen and practice.

Mr. Moore What's your name?
Adriana Adriana Moraes.
Mr. Moore Is that A-D-R-I-A-N-A?
Adriana Yes, that's right.
Mr. Moore And how do you spell your last name?
Adriana M-O-R-A-E-S.
Mr. Moore OK. Here's your card.

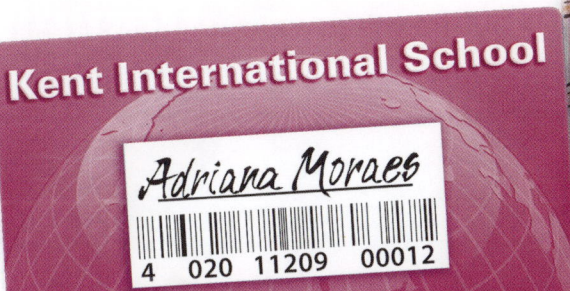

Names	
First names	**Last names**
Yoshi	Sato
Jenny	Wilson
Tyler	Foster
How do you spell your last name?	
M-O-R-A-E-S.	

B Complete the conversation with your own information. Then practice with a classmate.

A What's your name?
B _____
A How do you spell your last name?
B _____

4. Speaking

Learn to spell your classmates' last names.

You Hi! What's your last name?
Classmate . . . .
You How do you spell your last name?
Classmate . . . .

Back to School 11

UNIT 1 Get Connected

Read

A Read the article quickly. Write the last names of the three people in the article.

1. _____ 3. _____
2. _____

Meet Jayden, Amira, and Daniel!

Hi, friends! My name is Jayden. My last name is Hampton. **I like candy bars**, and I like basketball. Oh, and my nickname is Jay. What's your nickname?

Good afternoon! I'm Amira Moore. My nickname is Amy. My **dog's** name is Star. I like **sushi**! Nice to meet you. See you later.

Hello. I'm Daniel Reyes. My nickname is Dan. I like **music**, and I like school. I'm great today. How about you? How are you today?

More Vocabulary Practice? See page 122.

B 🎧 T.21 Read the article slowly. Check your answers in Part A.

C Circle the correct words to complete the sentences.

1. Jayden's last name is (Moore / (Hampton) / Reyes).
2. Jayden likes (basketball / school / sushi).
3. Amira's dog's name is (Reyes / Star / Moore).
4. Amira likes (sushi / candy bars / music).
5. Daniel's nickname is (Amy / Dan / Jay).
6. Daniel's (name / nickname / last name) is Reyes.

12 Unit 1

What's your name?

A 🎧 T.22 Kevin and Megan introduce themselves. Listen and write *True* or *False*. Then correct the false statements.

1. Megan is a new student. _True._ _____
2. Kevin's last name is Bartelsman. _____
3. Megan's first name is Jones. _____
4. Megan's nickname is Peg. _____
5. Kevin's nickname is Kev. _____

B What do you think? Write *I agree* or *I disagree* (don't agree).

1. Nicknames are cool. _____
2. I like my name. _____
3. My name is easy to spell. _____
4. My friend's name is easy to spell. _____

Listen

Your turn

A Complete the chart.

First name	
Last name	
Nickname	
School	
How are you today?	
I like . . .	

B Write about yourself to your new e-pal. Use the chart in Part A to help you.

Hello! My name is _____ My last name is _____

Write

Back to School 13

UNIT 1 Review

Language chart review

Personal information	Introductions
What's your name? 　**My name is** Emma. 　**I'm** Emma. **How do you spell** your name? 　E-M-M-A. **How are you** today? 　**Great!** 　**Fine**, thank you. 　**Not too good.**	Hi. **I'm** Emma. Andrew, **this is** Meg. Meg, **this is** Andrew.

What's = What is
I'm = I am

A Complete the conversations with the sentences in the box.

> ☑ Hello, Mr. McDonald. How are you?   ☐ Nice to meet you, too.
> ☐ Steven, this is Monica.   ☐ Not bad, thank you.

1. **A** _Hello, Mr. McDonald. How are you?_
   B Good, thanks. How about you, Caroline?
   A _____

2. **A** _____
   B Hi, Monica. Nice to meet you.
   C _____

B Match the conversations from Part A to the pictures. Write the numbers.

C Meet Leigh and Lee. Complete the conversations.

1
Hello. _What's_ your name?
My name _____ Leigh Jones.
Hi. _____ Lee, too.

2
How do you spell _____ name?
L-E-E. _____ about you?
L-E-I-G-H.

3
Hi, Mr. Garcia. _____ are you today?
Great, thanks.
_____ is my new friend, Leigh.

4
Hi, Leigh. _____ to meet you.
Nice to meet _____, too, Mr. Garcia.

D Circle the word in each box that is different. Then complete the message with the colored letter from that word.

(H**e**llo.)	Good morn**i**ng.	N**o**t bad.	D**a**vid
Good n**i**ght.	G**o**od-bye.	Gr**e**at.	J**o**hn
B**y**e.	Good **a**fternoon.	Th**a**nk you.	Anni**e**
Go**o**d-bye.	Good **e**vening.	F**i**ne.	W**i**lliam

S e e   y   u   l   t   r   !

Time for the Theme Project?
See page 126.

Back to School 15

Lesson 5

Teachers and friends

1. Vocabulary

A Listen to Tyler talk about his photo album. Number the pictures. Then listen again and practice.

T.23

This is my classmate, Jenny.

This is my best friend, Paulo.

This is my math teacher, Mr. Stern.

This is my science teacher, Ms. Davis.

This is my basketball coach, Mr. Diaz.

This is my computer lab partner, Sandra.

B Write about three people at your school.

Ms. Davis is my science teacher.

1. _____
2. _____
3. _____

UNIT 2 Favorite People

2. Language focus

A Tyler and his dad look at photos. Listen and practice.

Tyler Look, Dad, this is my new basketball coach.
Mr. Foster What's his name?
Tyler His name is Mr. Diaz.
Mr. Foster Who's this?
Tyler This is my computer lab partner. Her name is Sandra.
Mr. Foster And who's this?
Tyler Dad! This is Paulo – my best friend.

his / her
What's **his** name?
His name is Mr. Diaz.
What's **her** name?
Her name is Sandra.

Who's this?
Who's this?
This is my computer lab partner.
My computer lab partner.
Who's = Who is

B Complete the conversations. Listen and check. Then practice.

1. **Mr. Foster** _Who's_ (Who's / What's) this?
   Tyler My math teacher.
   Mr. Foster What's _____ (his / her) name?
   Tyler _____ (His / Her) name is Mr. Stern.

2. **Tyler** This is my classmate.
   Mr. Foster _____ (What's / Who's) her name?
   Tyler _____ (His / Her) name is Jenny.

3. **Mr. Foster** And _____ (who's / what's) this?
   Tyler My science teacher. _____ (His / Her) name is Ms. Davis.

3. Pronunciation Contractions with question words

A Listen. Notice the contractions *Who's* and *What's*. Then listen again and practice.

Who's this?   What's her name?   What's his name?

B Now practice the conversations in Exercise 2B.

Favorite People 17

Lesson 6: Favorite stars

1. Vocabulary

Look at the photos on Julia's Web site. Label the pictures with the words in the box. Then listen and practice.

- ☐ actor
- ☑ model
- ☐ soccer player
- ☐ TV star
- ☐ cartoon character
- ☐ singer
- ☐ tennis player

1. Gisele Bündchen — *model*
2. Eugenie Bouchard
3. Amazing Spider-Man
4. Neymar
5. Alicia Keys
6. Brad Pitt
7. Ryan Seacrest

2. Language focus

A Wendy, Julia, and Clare talk about their favorite stars. Listen and practice.

Wendy Who's this?
Julia Gisele Bündchen. She's my favorite model.
Clare And who's this?
Julia Neymar. He's my favorite soccer player.
Wendy So, who's your favorite actor?
Julia Brad Pitt. He's right here.
Clare Oh, I'm a Brad Pitt fan, too. I think he's cute.

He's / She's ...
He's my favorite soccer player.
She's my favorite model.
He's = He is   She's = She is

B Write about these stars from Julia's Web site. Then listen and check.

1. (Gisele Bündchen) _This is Gisele Bündchen. She's a model._
2. (Amazing Spider-Man) _____
3. (Eugenie Bouchard) _____
4. (Ryan Seacrest) _____
5. (Neymar) _____

3. Listening

Listen to students talk about their favorite stars. Check (✓) the correct stars.

1. ✓ actor   2. ☐ model   3. ☐ soccer player   4. ☐ cartoon character
   ☐ TV star   ☐ singer   ☐ tennis player   ☐ TV star

4. Speaking

Complete the chart with your favorite stars.
Then ask two classmates about their favorite stars.

	You	Classmate 1	Classmate 2
Actor	_____	_____	_____
Singer	_____	_____	_____
Cartoon character	_____	_____	_____

Who's your favorite ......?

My favorite ...... is ....

Favorite People 19

Lessons 5 & 6 Mini-review

1. Language check

A Dina introduces Olivia to Ryan. Complete the conversation. Then practice.

Dina Hi, Ryan. How _are_ (is / are) you?
Ryan Great, thanks.
Dina Ryan, _____ (this / she) is Olivia. _____ (He's / She's) my partner in science class.
Ryan Nice to meet _____ (you / she), Olivia.
Olivia Nice to meet you, too. _____ (What's / Who's) your partner in science class, Ryan?
Ryan Rebecca.
Olivia _____ (What's / Who's) her last name?
Ryan Johnson.
Olivia Really? She's _____ (my / your) best friend!

Olivia   Dina   Ryan

B Complete the sentences with *He's*, *She's*, *His*, or *Her*.

1. This is Luiz. _He's_ my partner in English class. _____ favorite class is science.

2. This is Lin. _____ my best friend. _____ favorite singer is Beyoncé.

3. Mr. Adams is my favorite teacher. _____ great. _____ first name is Ethan.

20 Unit 2

C Circle the correct words to complete the e-mail.

TO: raul.gm@cct.net
FROM: linda.nl@cct.net
SUBJECT: Hello!

Hi, Raul!

How are you? I'm fine.

This is (**my** / you) best friend. (Her / She) name is Mia.

(He's / She's) really nice. (What's / Who's) your best friend?

(What's / Who's) his or her name?

Mia's favorite actor is Chris Hemsworth. I think

(he's / his) a good actor. (He's / His) best movie is

Thor: The Dark World. (What's / Who's) your favorite star?

Your friend,

Linda

2. Listening

A Who is each person talking about? Listen and check (✓) the correct answers.

	An actor	A tennis player	A teacher	A best friend	A singer	A cartoon character
1.					✓	
2.						
3.						
4.						
5.						
6.						

B Now listen to the complete information. Check your answers.

Time for a Game?
See page 115.

Favorite People

Lesson 7 Birthdays

1. Numbers 0–20

A Listen to the numbers. Then practice.
T.33

0 zero (oh)	5 five	10 ten	15 fifteen	18 eighteen
1 one	6 six	11 eleven	16 sixteen	19 nineteen
2 two	7 seven	12 twelve	17 seventeen	20 twenty
3 three	8 eight	13 thirteen		
4 four	9 nine	14 fourteen		

B Listen and write the ages.
T.34

Today's birthdays

Name: Zach Shaw
Age: 17

Name: Hannah Kirby
Age: _____

Name: Carla Mendez
Age: _____

Name: Leo Garcia
Age: _____

Name: Lizzy Smith
Age: _____

Name: Dan Ito
Age: _____

C Look at Part B. Write words for the ages.

1. Zach is _seventeen_ .
2. Hannah is _____ .
3. Lizzy is _____ .
4. Carla and Dan are _____ .
5. Leo is _____ .

22 Unit 2

2. Language focus

A Joy is at Dan's birthday party. Listen and practice.

Joy Happy birthday, Dan!
How old are you today? Thirteen?
Dan No, I'm twelve. How old are you? Thirteen?
Joy No, I'm not thirteen. I'm only eleven. But my birthday is tomorrow.
Dan Really? Happy birthday!

How old . . . ?	
How old are you?	How old is she?
I'm twelve.	She's three.

He's not / She's not
He's not thirteen. He's twelve.
She's not four. She's only three.

B Look at Exercise 1B on page 22. Answer the questions. Then listen and check.

1. How old is Carla? Thirteen? *No, she's not thirteen. She's twelve.*
2. How old is Hannah? Twelve? _____
3. How old is Leo? Eleven? _____
4. How old is Lizzy? Six? _____
5. How old is Dan? Ten? _____
6. How old is Zach? Eighteen? _____

3. Listening

A How old are these people today? Write your guesses in the chart.

	Chris	Anna	Andy	Joshua
Your guess	eleven			
Correct age				

B Compare answers. Then listen and write the correct ages in the chart.

> How old is Chris? I think he's eleven.

> I think he's thirteen.

4. Speaking

Learn the ages of four of your classmates.

You How old are you, ... ?
Classmate I'm . . . . How old are you?
You I'm . . . .

Favorite People   23

Lesson 8: E-pals

1. Vocabulary

A Jenny and Paulo look at pictures of students and their e-pals. Where are they from? Listen and complete the sentences. Then listen again and practice.

1. Paulo is from _Brazil_.   His e-pal is from _Peru_.
2. Jenny is from _____.   Her e-pal is from _____.
3. Nicole is from _____. Her e-pal is from _____.
4. Tyler is from _____.   His e-pal is from _____.
5. Sandra is from _____. Her e-pal is from _____.
6. Yoshi is from _____.   His e-pal is from _____.

B Now draw lines to match the students with their e-pals.

Students
- Paulo, Brazil (age 12)
- Sandra, Mexico (age 12)

E-pals
- Mike, Canada (age 12)
- Miguel, Colombia (age 12)

2. Speaking

Talk about the people on the map.

- **You** Mike is from Canada.
- **Classmate 1** How old is he?
- **Classmate 2** He's 12.

24 Unit 2

3. Language focus

A Paulo and Jenny talk about e-pals. Listen and practice.

Paulo Hi, Jenny. Who's that?
Jenny That's Mike. He's my e-pal. He's 12.
Paulo Where's he from?
Jenny He's from Canada.
Paulo You're from Canada, too, right?
Jenny Canada? I'm not from Canada.
Paulo Really? Where are you from?
Jenny I'm from the U.S.
Paulo Oh, right. Sorry.

Where . . . from?
Where are you from?
I'm from the U.S.
Where's he from?
He's from Canada.
Where's = *Where is*
You're / I'm not
You're from Canada, right?
I'm not from Canada.
I'm from the U.S.
You're = *You are*
the U.S. = *the United States*

Jenny, the U.S. (age 13)
Tyler, the U.S. (age 12)
Nicole, Canada (age 12)
Yoshi, Japan (age 12)
Maria, Peru (age 13)
Emma, Australia (age 13)
Claudio, Venezuela (age 14)
Lina, Portugal (age 13)

B Complete the conversation. Listen and check. Then practice.

Paulo Here's a photo of my e-pal, Maria.
Jenny She's cute! _____ she from?
Paulo _____ from Peru.
Jenny Peru? You're from Peru, too, right?
Paulo Jenny, I'm _____ from Peru. I'm from Brazil.
Jenny I'm just kidding! I know that.

Favorite People 25

UNIT 2 Get Connected

Read

A Read the article quickly. Check (✓) the words you find.

☐ 1. model   ☐ 3. singer   ☐ 5. cartoon character
☐ 2. TV star   ☐ 4. actor   ☐ 6. a soccer player

SAM'S FAVORITES

Samantha Carter – "Sam"

This is Bubbles, my favorite cartoon character. She's from Townsville – a fictional city in the U.S. She is one of The Powerpuff Girls. Bubbles is very **cute**.

Here's a photo of Shakira. She's my favorite singer. She's not from Mexico. She's from Colombia. Her nickname is Shaki. I think she's **beautiful**!

Ellen Page is 29. She isn't from the U.S. She's from Canada. She's my favorite actor. She likes basketball and soccer. Her soccer nickname is "Peeps."

Here's my favorite TV star. His name is Kunal Nayyar, and he's from India. He's Raj on the **TV show** The Big Bang Theory. I like Kunal. He's great and so is The Big Bang Theory.

Meet my best friend, Tim. He's from Australia, not the U.S. He's 13. His favorite class is math and his favorite **sports** are tennis and basketball.

More Vocabulary Practice? See page 122.

B 🎧 T.41 Read the article slowly. Check your answers in Part A.

C Are these statements true or false? Write *True* or *False*. Then correct the false statements.

1. Shakira is from Mexico.   _False._   _She's from Colombia._
2. Shakira's nickname is Shaki.   _____
3. Kunal is a cartoon character.   _____
4. Bubbles is very cute.   _____
5. Ellen Page isn't from Canada.   _____
6. Tim is Sam's favorite TV star.   _____

She's so cute!

Listen

A 🎧 T.42 Andrew and Manny talk about Andrew's new science partner. Listen and circle the correct words.

1. Isabel is Andrew's new (classmate / (science partner) / best friend).
2. Isabel is from (Peru / Portugal / Brazil).
3. Isabel's nickname is (Cute / Manny / Izzy).
4. Andrew's favorite singer is (Jesse McCartney / Isabel / Justin Timberlake).
5. Andrew thinks (SpongeBob / Isabel / Spider-Man) is awesome.

B Are these statements true or false for you? Write *True* or *False*. Then correct the false statements. Use your own information.

1. Thirteen (13) is a good age. _____
2. Justin Timberlake is a great singer. _____
3. Cartoons are funny. _____
4. SpongeBob is a good cartoon character. _____

Your turn

Write

A Complete the chart.

Who's your . . . ?	Name	Where's he / she from?	I think he / she is . . .
favorite classmate			
favorite teacher			
favorite coach			
favorite e-pal			

B Write about your favorite people. Use the chart in Part A to help you.

My best friend is _____. He's / She's from _____. I think _____.

Favorite People   27

UNIT 2 Review

Language chart review

The verb be			
Wh- questions	**Statements**	**I'm / He's / She's . . .**	**My / His / Her . . .**
How old are you?	I'm 16. I'm not 18. You're 15. You're not 14.	I'm a singer. He's a model. She's a teacher.	My name is Carla. His name is Steven. Her name is Ms. Kelly.
Where's he from?	He's from Brazil. He's not from Peru.	He's = He is She's = She is	
Where's she from?	She's from Canada. She's not from the U.S.		
Who's this?	This is my best friend.		
Where's = Where is Who's = Who is	You're = You are		

A Complete the sentences in the comic book with *I'm*, *he's*, *she's*, *my*, *his*, or *her*.

> It's the year 2075. People can travel around the world in minutes. Kate meets her friends at the Global Café.

Kate and Her Global Friends

Hi. _My_ name is Kate. I'm thirteen, and _____ from Australia.

This is _____ best Global friend. _____ name is Felicia. _____ from Mexico, and _____ fourteen.

This is Carlos. _____ from Peru. _____ my Global computer partner. _____ favorite class is computer science.

28 Unit 2

B Complete the questions with *Who, What, Where,* or *How.*
Then match each question to the correct answer.

1. _How_ old is Kate? _f_
2. _____ is she from? ____
3. _____ is her best friend? ____
4. _____ old is Felicia? ____
5. _____ is Carlos from? ____
6. _____ is the name of the café? ____

a. She's from Mexico.
b. Felicia.
c. He's from Peru.
d. She's fourteen.
e. Global Café.
f. She's thirteen.

C Read about these comic book characters. Then write about them.

Name: Seth Strong
Age: 15
Country: Canada

Name: Carla Cool
Age: 17
Country: Colombia

Name: Akio Adventure
Age: 12
Country: Japan

1. _His name is Seth._
   He's _____
   He's from _____

2. _____
   _____
   _____

3. _____
   _____
   _____

D Look again at Part C. Correct these sentences.

1. Seth is sixteen.   _Seth is not sixteen. He's fifteen._
2. Seth is from the U.S.   _____
3. Carla's last name is Strong.   _____
4. Carla is from Venezuela.   _____
5. Akio is from Portugal.   _____
6. Akio is twenty.   _____

Time for the Theme Project?
See page 127.

Favorite People 29

Lesson 9: What a mess!

1. Vocabulary

A Matt and Tara are home from school. Look at the picture and write the names of the items. Use the words in the box. Then listen and practice.

T.43

☐ address book ☐ bag   ☐ brush   ☐ eraser ☐ notebook ☐ pencil case
☑ backpack   ☐ book   ☐ camera ☐ hat   ☐ pen   ☐ umbrella

1. backpack
2. _____
3. _____
4. _____
5. _____
6. _____
7. _____
8. _____
9. _____
10. _____
11. _____
12. _____

B Look at Part A. Listen to Tara and Matt. Are their statements true or false? Write *T* (true) or *F* (false).

T.44

1. Tara *T*   2. Matt ____   3. Tara ____   4. Matt ____   5. Tara ____

UNIT 3 Everyday Things

2. Language focus

A The living room is a mess. Listen and practice.

Mrs. Price Matt!
Matt Yes, Mom?
Mrs. Price Look at your things! What a mess!
Matt My things? This is Tara's pen, and that's her book.
Tara Yes, but that's Matt's hat, and . . .

This is / That's + possessive

This is Tara's pen.

That's Matt's hat.

That's = That is

B Complete the sentences with *This is* or *That's*. Then listen and check.

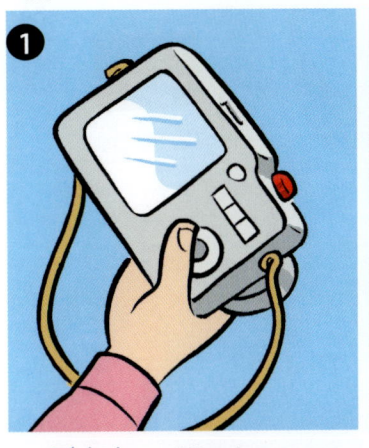

1.
This is Matt's camera.
That's his pencil case.

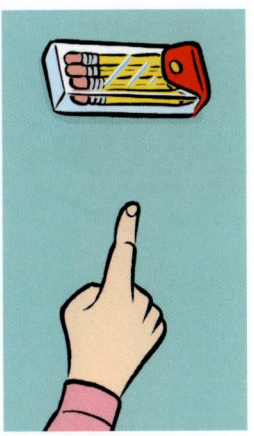

2.
_____ Matt's notebook.
_____ his umbrella.

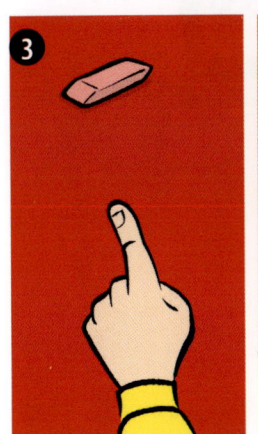

3.
_____ Tara's eraser.
_____ her book.

4.
_____ Tara's address book.
_____ her brush.

3. Speaking

Talk about your classmates' things.

This is Roberto's pencil case.

That's Anna's . . . .

Everyday Things 31

Lesson 10 Cool things

1. Vocabulary

A Complete the sentences with the words in the box. Then listen and practice.

- ☐ an alarm clock
- ☐ a cell phone
- ☐ an MP3 player
- ☐ a TV (television)
- ☐ a calculator
- ☐ a laptop
- ☐ a desktop computer
- ☑ a video game

1 This is _a video game_. That's _____. **2** This is _____. That's _____.

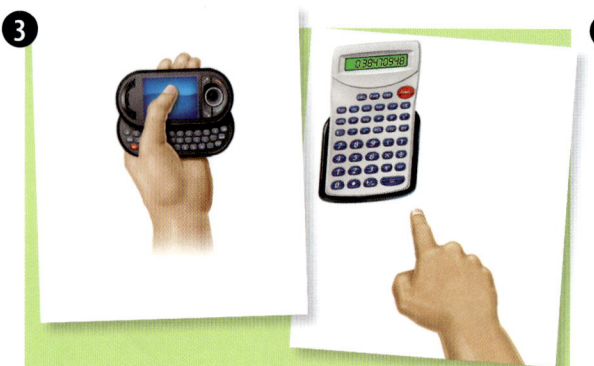

3 This is _____. That's _____. **4** This is _____. That's _____.

B Write *a* or *an* before each word.

1. _an_ address book
2. ____ brush
3. ____ camera
4. ____ pencil case
5. ____ eraser
6. ____ hat
7. ____ umbrella
8. ____ backpack

a / an

a + consonant
  a TV
  a cell phone

an + vowel sound
  an alarm clock
  an MP3 player

C Listen to the sounds. What do you hear? Who can answer first?

That's an alarm clock.

32 Unit 3

2. Language focus

A Sandra and Jenny look at interesting things. Listen and practice.

What's this / that?	
What's this?	**What's that?**
It's a calculator.	**It's** an old video game.
It's = It is	

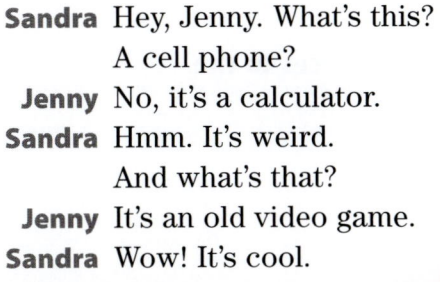

Sandra Hey, Jenny. What's this? A cell phone?
Jenny No, it's a calculator.
Sandra Hmm. It's weird. And what's that?
Jenny It's an old video game.
Sandra Wow! It's cool.

B Complete the conversation with the words in the box. Listen and check. Then practice.

- ☐ a   ☐ cool   ☐ that's   ☐ what's
- ☐ an   ☐ it's   ☑ this

Liz Hey, what's ___this___?
Ted It's _____ new tablet.
Liz Wow! It's _____ .
Ted Yeah. _____ also _____ e-book reader.
Jill Really? And _____ that?
Ted Oh, _____ a piano keyboard.
Jill Hmm . . . wireless piano keyboard?
Ted Yes. It's a really cool tablet.

3. Listening

Listen to the conversations. Circle the correct things.

1. a TV / a laptop
2. a calculator / a cell phone
3. a cell phone / a video game
4. an alarm clock / an MP3 player

Everyday Things

Lessons 9 & 10 Mini-review

1. Language check

A Check (✓) *a* or *an* for each sentence. Then match the sentences to the correct picture.

	a	an	Picture
1. This is ___ eraser.	☐	✓	*d*
2. It's ___ pen.	☐	☐	___
3. That's ___ TV.	☐	☐	___
4. It's ___ laptop.	☐	☐	___
5. This is ___ MP3 player.	☐	☐	___
6. That's ___ umbrella.	☐	☐	___

B These classmates are at the Museum of Technology. What do they say? Write sentences with *This is* or *That's*.

1. Vera: _That's a TV._

2. Jerry: _____

3. Lisa: _____

4. Miguel: _____

2. Listening

Are these things Joe's or Suzanne's? Listen and write *J* (Joe) or *S* (Suzanne).

T.52

1. _J_

2. _____

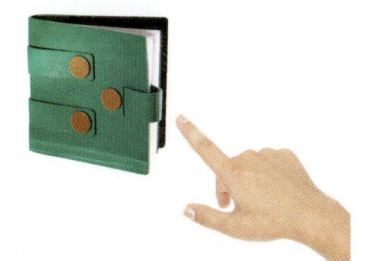

3. _____

4. _____

5. _____

6. _____

Time for a Game?
See page 116.

Everyday Things

Lesson 11: Favorite things

1. Vocabulary

A Label the photos of Nicole's and Yoshi's favorite things with the words in the box. Then listen and practice.

- ☑ bicycle
- ☐ comic books
- ☐ posters
- ☐ trading cards
- ☐ T-shirts
- ☐ watch

1. bicycle
2.
3.
4.
5.
6.

B What are your favorite things? Tell your classmates.

> My favorite things are my ...., my ...., and my ....

2. Pronunciation — Plural nouns

A Study the pronunciation chart. Then listen and practice.

No extra syllables	Extra syllable
book → books bag → bags	watch → watches case → cases

B Listen. Which plural nouns have extra syllables? Circle them.

1. hats
2. games
3. (coaches)
4. friends
5. brushes
6. boxes

3. Language focus

A There's a charity drive at school. Listen and practice. Then study the language chart.

Mr. Mori Hi, Paul. Tell me about your things. What are these?
Paul They're my favorite T-shirts. They're too small now.
Mr. Mori Oh, they're nice. And what are those?
Paul Those are my old watches.
Mr. Mori They're cool. Thanks, Paul.

What are these / those?	
What are these?	**What are those?**
These are T-shirts.	**Those are** watches.
They're T-shirts.	**They're** watches.

They're = They are

B Look at the picture. Complete the conversation with *these*, *those*, or *they're*. Listen and check. Then practice.

Ms. Garcia So, what are ___those___, Monica?
Monica They're my comic books.
Ms. Garcia Hmm. _____ very interesting.
Monica _____ are my trading cards.
Ms. Garcia Oh, they're nice. What's in this box?
Monica _____ my old books.
Ms. Garcia Monica, _____ your English books!
Monica Yeah. They're from last year.

4. Speaking

Look at the things in the pictures on pages 36 and 37. Ask and answer questions.

What are these?   They're T-shirts.   What's this?   It's a / an ....

Everyday Things

Lesson 12: Where is it?

1. Vocabulary

A David is late for school. Where are his things?
Match the two parts of each sentence.
Then listen and practice.

1. David's books are _f_
2. His basketball is ___
3. His brush is ___
4. His watch is ___
5. His bag is ___
6. The photos are ___

a. under the bed.
b. in the wastebasket.
c. on the wall.
d. on the dresser.
e. next to the chair.
f. on the desk.

in
under
next to
on

B Look at David's room. Complete the sentences with
in, *under*, *next to*, or *on*.

1. David's alarm clock is __on__ the dresser.
2. His hat is ___ the bed.
3. His wastebasket is ___ the desk.
4. His posters are ___ the wall.
5. His books are ___ the camera.
6. His pencils are ___ the bag.

the
the desk
the books

38 Unit 3

2. Language focus

Complete the conversation. Listen and check. Then practice.
T.59

David Dad! I'm late. Where are my pencils? They're not in my pencil case.
Mr. Evans They're in your bag.
David OK, but where's my bag? It's not on the desk.
Mr. Evans It's under the bed.
David Oh, right. Thanks. Oh! _Where are_ my books? _____ in my bag!
Mr. Evans _____ next to your computer.
David And _____ my watch? _____ on the dresser.
Mr. Evans _____ in the wastebasket, David!

Where's / Where are . . . ?
Where's my bag?
  It's under the bed.
Where are my pencils?
  They're in your bag.

It's not / They're not . . .
It's not on the desk.
They're not in my pencil case.

---

3. Listening

Where's the backpack? Listen and number the pictures.
T.60

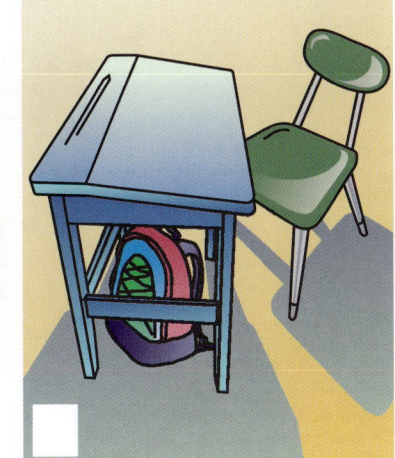

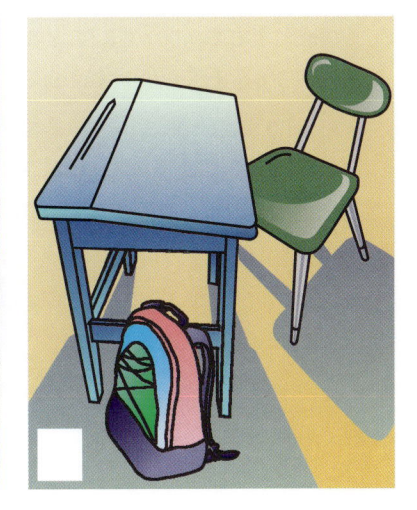

4. Speaking

Look at the picture on page 38. Make true and false statements. Your classmate says *Yes* or *No* and corrects the false statements.

You The bag is under the bed.
Classmate Yes.
You The books are next to the desk.
Classmate No. They're not next to the desk. They're on the desk.

Everyday Things

UNIT 3 Get Connected

Read

A Read the article quickly. Who's Maxie?

_____

A really cool tree house

Meet Pete. He's a really interesting **teenager**. This is his **virtual tree house**. It's really cool.

Look next to the desk. What's that? It's Pete's pet **spider**. Her name is Angelina. She's a very nice spider.

Where's the wastebasket? It's under the desk. Where's the laptop? It's on the desk. And there's a photo on the desk, too.

And who's that next to the chair? That's Coco. She's Pete's **cat**. She's great. And that's Maxie, Pete's dog. He's funny – he **smiles**!

Look at the wall. There's a poster and a clock on the wall. The poster is weird. It's of Pete's favorite band.

Pete's virtual tree house isn't a mess. Is your room a mess?

More Vocabulary Practice? See page 123.

B Read the article slowly. Check your answer in Part A. (T.61)

C Answer the questions.

1. Where's the spider? _It's / She's next to the desk._
2. Where's the wastebasket? _____
3. Where are the laptop and the photo? _____
4. Where's Coco? _____
5. Where are the clock and the poster? _____

It's in your bag!

Listen

A Tim and Katie talk about where Tim's MP3 player is. Listen and write *True* or *False*. Then correct the false statements.

1. Tim and Katie are late. _True._
2. Tim's MP3 player is in his bag. _____
3. Tim's cell phone is a calculator, too. _____
4. His video game is on the dresser. _____
5. A spider is on the bed. _____

B What do you think? Write *I agree* or *I disagree* (don't agree).

1. I think cell phones are great. _____
2. I think video games are interesting. _____
3. I think MP3 players are cool. _____
4. I think spiders are weird. _____

Your turn

Write

A Imagine a virtual classroom. Check (✓) the items in the classroom.

- ☐ bag   ☐ chair   ☐ computer   ☐ eraser   ☐ pen   ☐ TV
- ☐ books ☐ clock ☐ desk   ☐ notebook ☐ poster ☐ wastebasket

B Write about your virtual classroom. Use the words in Part A to help you.

This is my virtual classroom. There's a wastebasket next . . .

Everyday Things

UNIT 3 Review

Language chart review

this / that / these / those questions and statements a / an	
This is a camera. What's this? It's a camera. That's an address book. What's that? It's an address book.	These are pens. What are these? They're pens. Those are comic books. What are those? They're comic books.
That's = That is It's = It is	They're = They are
Possessive 's	
This is Paul's backpack. These are Eva's pencils.	

A Ben and Lee are at camp. Look at the picture. Then complete the conversation.

Lee Hey, Ben. What are _____those_____ (these / those) ?
Ben _____ (It's / They're) my favorite comic books.
Lee Oh, I see. _____ (Who's / What's) on the cover?
Ben _____ (He's / They're) my favorite superhero.
Lee And what's _____ (that / those) on the floor?
Ben It's _____ (a / an) sports magazine. I love soccer!
Lee And _____ (what's / who's) that?
Ben It's _____ (a / an) tablet.
Lee Wow! It's really nice. And what's _____ (this / that) in your backpack?
Ben _____ (It's / They're) my new camera.

B The names of seven more things are in the pencil. Circle them.
Then write them in the chart. Use *a* or *an* for the singular words.

televisionwatchescamerascellphoneumbrellastradingcardsbicycleaddressbook

Singular		Plural	
a television			

Language chart review

Where's / Where are...?		Prepositions
Where's my cell phone?	It's **not** in my bag. It's on the desk.	in on
Where are my books?	They're **not** next to my computer. They're under the bed.	next to under

C Look at the picture. Then correct the sentences.

1. The books are on the desk. _They're not on the desk. They're on the bed._
2. The pencils are next to the backpack. _____
3. The umbrella is next to the dresser. _____
4. The hat is on the bed. _____

D Look again at the picture in Part C. Write questions and answers about the other things.

1. **Q:** _Where's the basketball?_ **A:** _It's next to the dresser._
2. **Q:** _____ **A:** _____
3. **Q:** _____ **A:** _____
4. **Q:** _____ **A:** _____

Time for the Theme Project?
See page 128.

Everyday Things 43

Lesson 13: At the movies

1. Vocabulary

A Where are Jenny and her friends? Listen and match the two parts of each sentence.

> at
> at the newsstand

1. Jenny is _e_.
2. Tyler is ___.
3. Sandra is ___.
4. Nicole is ___.
5. Yoshi is ___.
6. Paulo is ___.

a. at the newsstand
b. at the Internet café
c. at the restaurant
d. at the bus stop
e. at the movie theater
f. at the shoe store

B Listen again and check your answers in Part A. Then practice.

2. Listening

Look at the photos in Exercise 1. Where are the people? Listen and number the places.

___ Internet café ___ newsstand _1_ restaurant
___ movie theater ___ shoe store ___ bus stop

UNIT 4 Around Town

3. Language focus

A Jenny is at the movie theater. All of her friends are late! Listen and practice.

Tyler Hello?
Jenny Tyler, this is Jenny. It's really late. Are you still at home?
Tyler No, I'm not.
Jenny Oh. Are you near the movie theater?
Tyler Yes, I am. I'm at the bus stop.
Jenny Well, please hurry. You're late!
Tyler OK. I'm sorry.

Are you . . . ?
Are you still at home?
Are you near the movie theater?
Yes, I am.
No, I'm not.

B Complete the conversations. Listen and check. Then practice.

1. **Sandra** Hello?
   Jenny Hi, Sandra. Where are you? Are ___you___ near the movie theater?
   Sandra Yes, I _____ . I'm at the shoe store.
   Jenny _____ you with Paulo?
   Sandra No, I'm _____ .
   Jenny OK. Hurry. It's late!

2. **Paulo** Hello?
   Jenny Hi, Paulo. You're late! _____ _____ near the movie theater?
   Paulo No, _____ _____ . I'm still at home.
   Jenny Oh, no, Paulo! Hurry!
   Paulo I'm kidding. I'm at the newsstand.

4. Speaking

Complete these questions. Then interview a classmate.

Are you . . . ?	Yes	No
Are you _____ years old? (*age*)	☐	☐
Are you a _____ player? (*sport*)	☐	☐
Are you a _____ fan? (*favorite star*)	☐	☐
Are you from _____ ? (*city* or *town*)	☐	☐

Are you 12 years old?

Yes, I am.

Lesson 14: Downtown

1. Vocabulary

A Look at the map. Complete the sentences. Then listen and practice.

1. The drugstore is ___on___ Jefferson Street.
2. The department store is _____ the movie theater.
3. The parking lot is _____ the movie theater.
4. The bank is _____ the restaurant and the shoe store.
5. The subway station is _____ the shoe store.
6. The park is _____ the school.

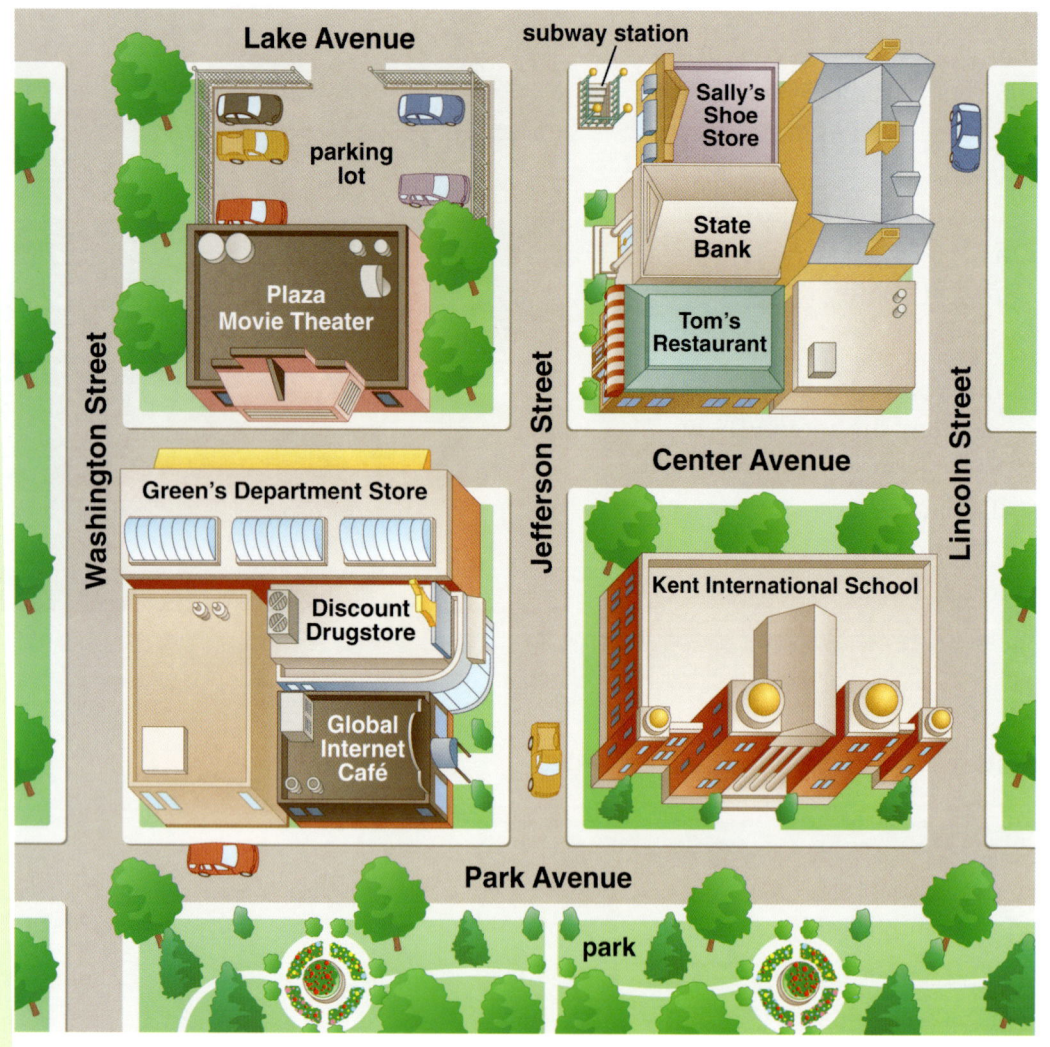

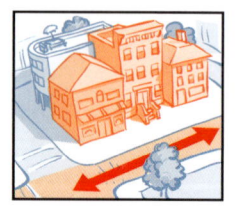

on

in front of

behind

across from

between

B Look at the places on the map. Make true and false statements. A classmate answers *True* or *False*.

> The parking lot is behind the movie theater.

> True.

46   Unit 4

2. Language focus

A Jackie and Lizzy are downtown. Listen and practice.

Jackie I'm hungry! Let's go to Tom's Restaurant.
Lizzy OK. Where is it?
Jackie I think it's on Park Avenue.
Lizzy Oh. Is it across from the Internet café?
Jackie No, it's not. It's next to the bank.
Lizzy But the bank is on Jefferson Street.
Jackie Uh-oh. I'm lost! Let's look at the map!

Is it . . . ?
Is it across from the Internet café?
Yes, it is.
No, it's not.

B Write questions about the map on page 46. Then practice with a classmate.

1. *Is the parking lot behind the shoe store?*
2. _____
3. _____
4. _____
5. _____

Is the parking lot behind the shoe store?

No, it's not. It's behind the movie theater.

3. Pronunciation Yes / No questions

Listen. Notice the intonation in the questions. Then listen again and practice.

A Is the school on Park Avenue?
B Yes, it is.

A Is the restaurant in front of the drugstore?
B No, it's not.

4. Speaking

Think of a place in your town or city. Your classmates guess the place. Use the correct intonation.

Classmate 1 Is it near the school?
You Yes, it is.
Classmate 2 Is it on Miller Avenue?
You No, it's not.
Classmate 3 Is it across from the school?
You Yes, it is.
Classmate 4 Is it the park?
You Yes, it is.

Around Town 47

Lessons 13 & 14 Mini-review

1. Language check

A Carlos and Anna are at a soccer game. Complete the conversations with *I am, I'm not, it is,* or *it's not*. Then practice.

Carlos Hi. Are you Anna Jones?
Anna Yes, _I am_ .
Carlos I'm in your science class.
Anna Oh, right . . . GO, TIGERS, GO!
Carlos Are you from Canada, Anna?
Anna Uh, no, _____ .
I'm from the U.S.
Carlos Are you on a soccer team?
Anna No, _____ . I'm just a fan. GO! GO!

(Ring! Ring!)

Carlos Anna, is that your cell phone?
Anna Oh! Yes, _____ . Thanks.

Anna Hello?
Mrs. Jones Anna, are you still at school?
Anna Uh, no, _____ .
A GOAL! YAY, TIGERS!
Mrs. Jones Anna, are you at the soccer field?
Anna Well, yes, _____ .
Is that OK?
Mrs. Jones No, _____ !
It's very late.
Anna But, Mom, . . .

B Complete these questions. Then practice with a classmate.

1. _Are_ you a soccer fan?
2. _____ you 12 years old?
3. _____ your English class interesting?
4. _____ you a good student?
5. _____ your school nice?
6. _____ your home near the school?

Are you a soccer fan?   No, I'm not.

48   Unit 4

C Look at the map. Then correct the mistakes in the e-mail.

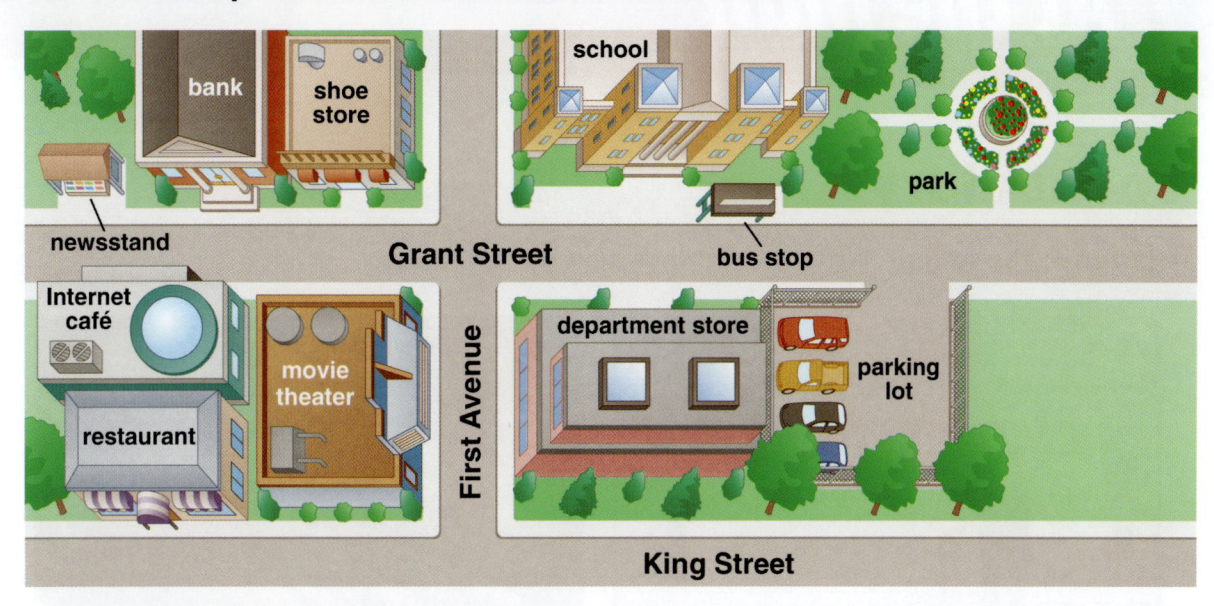

TO: donna.bee29840@cct.net
FROM: carlos.ft57365@cct.net
SUBJECT: Hi!

Hi, Donna!

How are you? I'm ~~on~~ *at* the Internet café. ~~Is~~ you still at home? Meet me ~~on~~ the department store in 15 minutes. It's ~~next to~~ the school, and it's ~~in front of~~ the parking lot.

See you soon,
Carlos

2. Listening

Look at the map in Exercise 1C. Listen and answer the questions. Write *No, it's not*, or *Yes, it is*.

1. No, it's not.
2. _____
3. _____
4. _____
5. _____
6. _____

Time for a Game?
See page 117.

Around Town 49

Lesson 15 — At the mall

1. Vocabulary

A Listen to the sounds. Write the number next to each place.
T.72

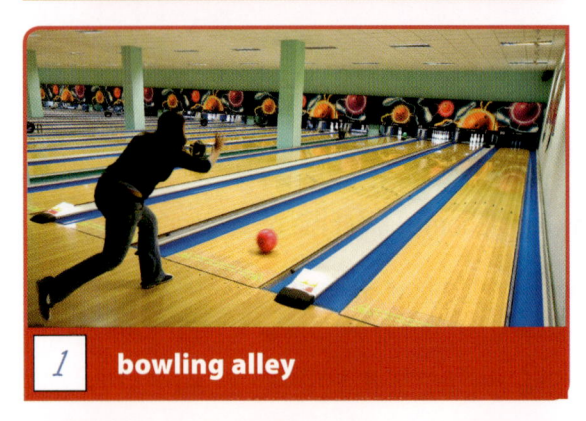

- [ ] skating rink
- [ ] music store
- [1] bowling alley
- [ ] candy store
- [ ] bookstore
- [ ] video arcade

B Listen and check. Then practice.
T.73

C Write about three of your favorite places.

My favorite music store is Virgo Beat Music.

1. _____
2. _____
3. _____

2. Language focus

A Yoshi and Paulo are at the mall with their friends. Listen and practice.

Yoshi Where is everybody?
Paulo Well, Tyler and Jenny are at the video arcade.
Yoshi What about Nicole? Is she there, too?
Paulo No, she's not. She's with Sandra.
Yoshi Oh. Are they at the skating rink?
Paulo No, they're not . . . They're at the movie theater.
Yoshi Oh, no! Let's hurry!

Is she / Are they . . . ?

Is she at the video arcade?
  Yes, she is.
  No, she's not.
Are they at the skating rink?
  Yes, they are.
  No, they're not.

B Read the conversation again. Complete the questions and then answer them. Then listen and check.

1. (Yoshi) _Is he_____ with Nicole?
   _No, he's not._____
2. (Jenny) _____ at the video arcade? _____
3. (Yoshi and Paulo) _____ at the mall? _____
4. (Tyler) _____ with Yoshi? _____
5. (Nicole) _____ with Tyler and Jenny? _____
6. (Nicole and Sandra) _____ at the skating rink? _____

3. Listening

A It's two hours later. Where are Paulo and his friends now? Listen and check (✓) the correct places.

	Candy store	Music store	Bookstore	Video arcade
Paulo	☐	☐	☐	☐
Jenny	☐	☐	☐	☐
Tyler	☐	☐	☐	☐
Nicole	☐	☐	☐	☐

B Compare answers with a classmate.

Is Paulo at the music store?

No, he's not. He's at the . . . .

Around Town 51

Lesson 16 Any suggestions?

1. Vocabulary

A Look at the people at the beach. Listen to the suggestions and practice.

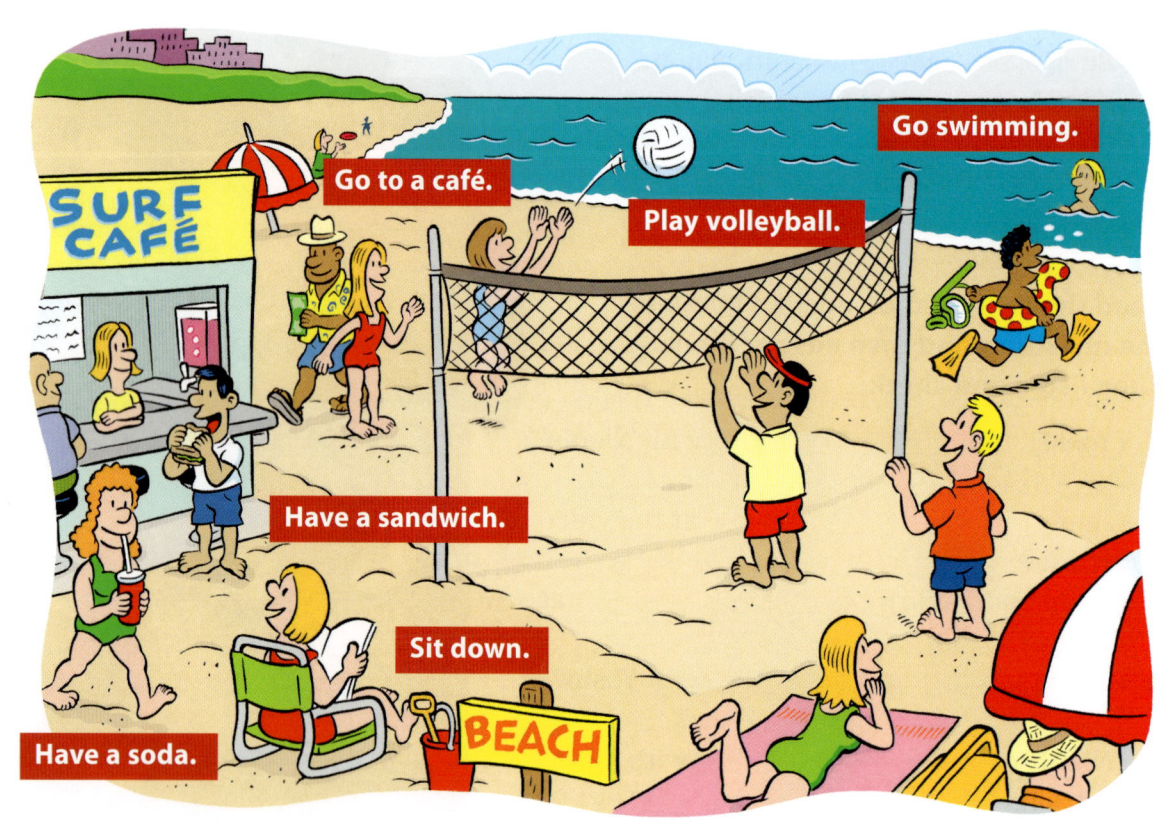

- Go to a café.
- Go swimming.
- Play volleyball.
- Have a sandwich.
- Sit down.
- Have a soda.

B Now write a suggestion for each person below. Use Part A to help you.

I'm **tired**.
Sit down.
_____

I'm **thirsty**.
_____
_____

I'm **hungry**.
_____
_____

I'm **hot**.
_____
_____

I'm **bored**.
_____
_____

2. Listening

What's the problem with these people? Listen and check (✓) the correct problem.

1. ☐ She's hot.
   ☐ She's tired.
2. ☐ He's bored.
   ☐ He's hungry.
3. ☐ They're thirsty.
   ☐ They're hungry.
4. ☐ She's tired.
   ☐ She's bored.

3. Language focus

A Matt and Chris are at the beach. Listen and practice.

Suggestions for others
Have a soda.
Suggestions for you + others
Let's go together.

Matt I'm thirsty.
Chris So go to a café, and have a soda.
Matt Good idea, but, um . . .
Chris What's wrong?
Matt Well, my money is at home.
Chris That's OK. I have money for two sodas. Let's go together.
Matt Great! Thanks, Chris!

B Complete the conversations with *go*, *have*, *sit*, or *play*. Listen and check. Then practice.

1. **A** Let's __play__ basketball.
   B But it's really hot.
   A Yeah – you're right. Let's _____ to the beach.
   B Good idea. Let's _____ swimming.

2. **A** I'm tired.
   B So _____ down.
   A OK. But I'm thirsty, too.
   B Then _____ to a café, and _____ a soda.

3. **A** Let's _____ a sandwich. I'm hungry.
   B Well, I'm not really hungry, but I am thirsty!
   A Oh. So _____ a soda.
   B OK. Let's _____ to a café.

4. **A** I'm really bored.
   B Me, too. Let's _____ to a video arcade.
   A But my money is at home.
   B Then let's _____ tennis in the park.
   A OK.

4. Speaking

Make suggestions. Use your own information or ideas.

I'm . . . .   So . . . .   I'm . . . .   Me, too. Let's . . . .

Around Town 53

UNIT 4 Get Connected

Read

A Read the Web site information quickly. Write the names of three places at West Edmonton Mall.

1. _____ 3. _____
2. _____

West Edmonton Mall

Welcome to the **biggest** mall in North America! We have interesting things for everybody.

Are you bored? Play **paintball** at Mad Existence Paintball. It's messy and it's weird, but it's very cool.

Are you hot? Go to the World Waterpark and play on the **waterslides**. It's across from the movie theaters.

Are you hungry and thirsty? Go to Jungle Jim's restaurant. It's on Bourbon Street. Sit down in the **jungle** and have a sandwich and a soda.

Look around the stores here, too! Are you a soccer fan? Go to Soccer Freak for your favorite soccer things. It's behind Sears department store. Or go to Comic King and look at comic books for your comic book collection. They have everybody's favorite comic books.

So hurry to Edmonton Mall – we have an **amusement park**, too!

B 🎧 T.81 Read the article slowly. Check your answers in Part A.

C Answer the questions.

1. Is the West Edmonton Mall in South America? _No, it's not._
2. Is paintball a game? _____
3. Are the movie theaters across from the World Waterpark? _____
4. Is Jungle Jim's a soccer store? _____
5. Is Soccer Freak in front of the department stores? _____
6. Are the comic books in Soccer Freak? _____

More Vocabulary Practice? See page 123.

I'm so bored!

Listen

A 🎧 T.82 **Judy and Anna talk about going to the mall. Listen and answer the questions.**

1. Are Anna and Judy at the mall? _No, they're not._
2. Is George's restaurant behind the video arcade? _____
3. Is Paul at the video arcade? _____
4. Is the music store between the video arcade and the bookstore? _____
5. Where's the bank? _____

B **What do you think? Write *I agree* or *I disagree* (don't agree).**

1. I think malls are fun. _____
2. I think video arcades are cool. _____
3. I think bookstores are interesting. _____
4. I think music stores are great. _____

Your turn

Write

A **What are your four favorite places in your neighborhood or mall? Where are they? Complete the chart.**

Place	Where is it?
Example: Nick's Video Arcade	across from the school
1.	
2.	
3.	
4.	

B **Write sentences about three or four of the places in your neighborhood or mall. Use the chart in Part A to help you.**

In my neighborhood, my favorite _____ is _____ _____. It's _____. It's really cool.

Around Town 55

UNIT 4 Review

Language chart review

Yes / No questions and short answers with be			Prepositions
Are you near the restaurant?	Yes, **I am**.	No, **I'm not**.	on
Is Yoshi at the video arcade?	Yes, **he is**.	No, **he's not**.	in front of
Is Sandra with Tyler?	Yes, **she is**.	No, **she's not**.	across from
Is the café near the movie theater?	Yes, **it is**.	No, **it's not**.	behind
Are Jenny and Paulo at the café?	Yes, **they are**.	No, **they're not**.	between

A Write questions with the correct forms of *be*. Then look at the picture, and answer the questions.

1. the school / behind the park

   Q: *Is the school behind the park?*   A: *No, it's not.*

2. the bicycles / behind the school

   Q: _____   A: _____

3. the soccer field / across from the park

   Q: _____   A: _____

4. the parking lot / in front of the school

   Q: _____   A: _____

5. the school / between the tennis courts and the soccer field

   Q: _____   A: _____

6. the school / on Clinton Street

   Q: _____   A: _____

B Look at the pictures. Complete the questions and answers.

1. **Q:** _Are they_ at the restaurant?
   A: _Yes, they are._

2. **Q:** _____ at the movie theater?
   A: _____

3. **Q:** _____ at the newsstand?
   A: _____

4. **Q:** _____ at the café?
   A: _____

5. **Q:** _____ at the bus stop?
   A: _____

Language chart review

Suggestions for others	Suggestions for you + others
Play volleyball.	**Let's go** swimming.
Sit down.	**Let's have** a sandwich.
Have a soda.	**Let's sit** down.

C Write a suggestion for each situation. Use the expressions in the box or your own ideas.

☐ go ☐ go swimming ☑ have a soda ☐ play a video game ☐ sit down

1. You and your friends are thirsty. _Let's have a soda._
2. Your brother is tired. _____
3. You and your sister are late for a movie. _____
4. Your friend is hot. _____
5. You and your friends are bored. _____

Time for the Theme Project? See page 129.

Lesson 17: My family

1. Numbers 21–100

🎧 **Listen to the numbers. Then practice.**
T.83

21 twenty-one	22 twenty-two	23 twenty-three
24 twenty-four	25 twenty-five	26 twenty-six
27 twenty-seven	28 twenty-eight	29 twenty-nine

| 30 thirty | 40 forty | 50 fifty | 60 sixty | 70 seventy | 80 eighty | 90 ninety | 100 one hundred |

2. Vocabulary

🎧 **A** Meet Sonia's family. Listen and practice.
T.84

This is my **sister**, Jen. She's 21. This is my **brother**, Eddie. He's 15.

These are my **grandparents**. My **grandfather** is 74. My **grandmother** is 67.

My name is Sonia. I'm 13.

This is my **cousin**, Mitch. He's 13, like me.

These are my **parents**. My **father** is 50. His name is Ned. My **mother** is 46. Her name is Claire.

This is my **uncle**, Ron, and my **aunt**, Sheila. He's 39 and she's 38.

B Complete these sentences about Sonia's family.

1. Sonia's ___mother___ is 46.
2. Her father is _____ .
3. Her _____ is 13.
4. Her aunt is _____ .
5. Her _____ is 15.
6. Her sister is _____ .
7. Her _____ are 67 and 74.
8. Her _____ is 39.

UNIT 5 Family and Home

3. Language focus

A Meet Sonia's cousin. Listen and practice.

have / has
I **have** three cousins.
I **have** no brothers or sisters.
She **has** a brother and a sister.
He **has** no brothers.

cousin → cousins
child → children

I'm Mitch. I'm Sonia's cousin. Sonia has a brother and a sister, so I have three cousins. But I have no brothers or sisters – I'm an only child.

B Complete the sentences with *have* or *has*. Then listen and check.

My name is Ron. I'm Sonia's uncle. I _have_ one sister. Her name is Claire. She's Sonia's mother. She _____ three children – Jen, Eddie, and Sonia. I _____ one child, Mitch.

I'm Sonia's grandmother. I _____ two children – Claire and Ron. Claire _____ three children. Ron _____ one child.

4. Speaking

A Complete the information for yourself. Write numbers. Then complete the information about a classmate.

Relative	You
brother(s)	
sister(s)	
cousin(s)	
aunt(s)	
uncle(s)	

I have two brothers.

I have no brothers.

Relative	Classmate
brother(s)	
sister(s)	
cousin(s)	
aunt(s)	
uncle(s)	

B Tell the class one thing about you and your classmate.

I have two brothers. Maria has no brothers.

Family and Home

Lesson 18: Family reunion

1. Vocabulary

A Read about Sally's family. Then listen and practice.

That's my brother, Tom. He's **smart**. He's **thin**.

Those are my cousins. Henry is **handsome**. Pam is **shy**, and she's **pretty**.

That's my grandfather. He's very **friendly**.

That's my mother. She's **tall**. My father is **short**.

Aunt Edna is on the chair. She's **funny** and a little **crazy**.

B Read about Sally's family again. What words describe the people? Write the words in the correct columns.

Appearance	Personality
handsome	friendly

60 Unit 5

2. Language focus

A Sally and Dan talk about her family. Complete the conversation. Listen and check. Then practice.

T.88

> **Sally** That's Pam. She's my cousin.
> **Dan** What's she like?
> **Sally** She's shy and . . .
> **Dan** She's very pretty.
> **Sally** Yes, I know, Dan.
> **Dan** What's your brother _____ ?
> **Sally** Tom? Oh, _____ smart.
> **Dan** And your Aunt Edna? _____ she _____ ?
> **Sally** Well, _____ really funny and a little _____ , too!

> **What's . . . like?**
> What's Pam like?
> She's shy.

B Complete the chart about two members of your family. Then answer a classmate's question about those family members.

Family member	Appearance	Personality
sister	tall	shy

> Sister. What's your sister like? She's tall and shy.

3. Pronunciation Final y

T.89

Listen to the final *y* in these words. Circle the word that sounds different. Then listen again and practice.

craz**y**   funn**y**   prett**y**   sh**y**   friendl**y**   reall**y**

4. Listening

T.90

A What else is true about Sally's family? Listen and match the two parts of each sentence.

1. Sally's mother is tall and ____   a. funny.
2. Sally's cousin, Henry, is handsome and ____   b. a little crazy.
3. Sally's grandfather is friendly and ____   c. thin.
4. Sally's father is short and really ____   d. smart.

B Now ask and answer questions about Sally's family.

> What's Sally's mother like?   She's tall and . . . .

Family and Home

Lessons 17 & 18 Mini-review

1. Language check

A Write the numbers.

1. 31 _thirty-one_
2. 45 _____
3. 100 _____
4. 53 _____
5. 78 _____
6. 24 _____
7. 96 _____
8. 60 _____
9. 82 _____
10. 27 _____
11. 33 _____
12. 86 _____

B Correct the sentences about Jordan's family.

NAME	AGE	WHO?
Jordan	12	me!
Lori	49	mother
Chris	52	father
Jill	15	sister
Jeremiah	24	brother

1. Jordan has ~~no brothers~~. _one brother_
2. His father is 55.
3. Jacob is his father.
4. His brother is 42.
5. Jill is his aunt.
6. His uncle is 49.

62 Unit 5

C Nicole talks to Yoshi about her family. Complete the sentences with *have* or *has*.

I _have_ a very big family. I _____ four sisters and three brothers. My mother _____ three brothers, too. My father _____ no brothers, but he _____ five sisters. I _____ 18 cousins. It's great!

D Compare your family to Nicole's family. Tell your classmates.

> Nicole has four sisters. I have no sisters.

2. Listening

A Now listen to Nicole describe three members of her family. Label the photos.

☐ Robert   ☐ Andrew   ☐ John

_____   _____   _____

B Complete the chart with information about three members of your family. Then tell your classmates.

Name	Family member	Age	Description
Peter	cousin	16	tall, thin, very smart

> My cousin's name is Peter. He's 16. He's . . .

Time for a Game?
See page 118.

Family and Home 63

Lesson 19: My new city

1. Vocabulary

A Look at the words in the photos. Listen and practice.

B Tyler's friend Mary lives in San Francisco now. Look at the photos, and complete the sentences about her new neighborhood.

1. ✓ noisy
2. ✓ quiet
3. ✓ big
4. ☐ small
5. ✓ old
6. ☐ new
7. ✓ happy
8. ☐ sad

Dear Tyler,
　San Francisco is great, but it's really _noisy_. My neighborhood isn't noisy — it's nice and very _quiet_. Across the street is a park. Next to my apartment is a _big_ mall with a lot of stores. Behind the mall is a _____ store with cool things.
　My school is really nice. It's very _old_. But inside, the computers, desks, and classrooms are _____.
　I'm really _happy_ in San Francisco. But sometimes I'm _____ — I miss my friends a lot!

　　　　　Write soon!
　　　　　Mary

C Tell your classmates about your neighborhood.

　My neighborhood is quiet.

Unit 5

2. Language focus

Tyler sends a message to Mary. Complete Tyler's message with *we're*, *they're*, *our*, or *their*. Listen and check. Then practice.

> **We're / They're; Our / Their**
> **We're** happy for you.
> **They're** from Canada.
>
> **Our** neighbors are very nice.
> **Their** last name is Martel.
>
> We're = We are   They're = They are

Dear Mary,

Thanks for your message. We miss you, too. But _____we're_____ happy for you. San Francisco is a great city.

The Martels live in your house now. _____ from Canada. _____ family is big. _____ all very nice. Nicole Martel and I are in the same English class. _____Our_____ English teacher is her father, Mr. Martel!

Nicole is also on my basketball team. _____ team is really great this year. _____ number one! Two players are from Brazil. _____ names are Carlos and Sergio. _____ really good.

Write soon. I miss you a lot!

Tyler

3. Listening

A The Martels talk about where they live. Listen and check (✓) the correct words.

1. the city	☐ nice	✓ big	✓ noisy
2. the neighborhood	☐ pretty	☐ quiet	☐ small
3. the neighbors	☐ happy	☐ quiet	☐ friendly
4. the house	☐ small	☐ nice	☐ new
5. the school	☐ big	☐ small	☐ noisy

B Now compare where you live to where the Martels live. Write three sentences.

Their city is big. Our city is small.

1. _____
2. _____
3. _____

Family and Home 65

Lesson 20 — At home

1. Vocabulary

A Which room is Brandon in? Listen and write the numbers.

- bedroom (1)
- bathroom
- living room
- kitchen
- garage
- dining room
- yard

B Listen and check. Then practice.

C Where are these things? Answer the questions.

1. Where are Brandon's posters?   _They're in the bedroom._
2. Where is his bicycle?   _____
3. Where are his comic books?   _____
4. Where is his backpack?   _____
5. Where is his hat?   _____
6. Where are his shoes?   _____

Unit 5

2. Language focus

A Match the homes to the correct texts. Listen and check. Then practice.

T.97

> **It has . . .**
> **It has** a small yard.
> **It has** three bedrooms.

☐ This is my grandparents' house. It's in the country. It has three bedrooms. It has a small yard.

☐ Our apartment is small, but it's very nice. It has two bedrooms and one bathroom. It has a big kitchen and a nice living room.

☐ My friend has a very big house. It has five bedrooms and three bathrooms! It also has a big garage.

B What's your home like? Write sentences with *It's* and *It has*.

_____
_____
_____
_____

3. Speaking

A What's your dream home like? Check (✓) your ideas.

My dream home is . . .
☐ a house.
☐ an apartment.

It's . . .
☐ in the city.
☐ in the country.

It's . . .
☐ big.
☐ small.

It has . . .
☐ a living room.
☐ a dining room.
☐ bathroom(s).
☐ bedroom(s).

It has . . . , too.
☐ a yard
☐ a garage
☐ a kitchen
☐ a/an _____

The neighborhood is . . .
☐ noisy.
☐ quiet.
☐ nice.

B Now tell your classmates.

> My dream home is a house. It's in the country. It's . . .

Family and Home

UNIT 5 Get Connected

Read

A Read the article quickly. Check (✓) the words you find.

☐ 1. brothers   ☐ 3. cousins   ☐ 5. parents   ☐ 7. fathers
☐ 2. aunts   ☐ 4. mother   ☐ 6. grandparents   ☐ 8. sisters

A Very Big Family

The Williams family is very big. Mary and George Williams have 11 children – 7 girls and 4 boys. The **youngest** is Mina. She's six. The **oldest** is Elizabeth. She's 35.

Elizabeth lives in a **different** city and she has a little girl.

Bernard, the oldest boy, also lives in a different city and has a little boy. So, Mary and George are parents and grandparents now. Elizabeth's and Bernard's children are **lucky** – they have a lot of aunts and uncles. What about the children still at home? They're not just brothers and sisters, but friends and classmates, too. They go to school together in their house – they're **homeschooled**. Their mother is their teacher. They really like sports. They **run**, play soccer, and play volleyball together. They're a big, happy family.

More Vocabulary Practice? See page 124.

B 🎧 T.98 Read the article slowly. Check your answers in Part A.

C Are these statements true or false? Write *True* or *False*. Then correct the false statements.

1. The family's last name is Foster. *False.* *The family's last name is Williams.*
2. The oldest sister is 35. _____
3. Mina lives in a different city. _____
4. Elizabeth's and Bernard's children aren't lucky. _____
5. The Williams children's school is their home. _____
6. The Williams family likes sports. _____

Twelve cousins!

Listen

A Matt and Dave talk about their families. Listen and circle the correct words.

T.99

1. Dave has a really (friendly / small / (big)) family.
2. Dave has (twelve / seven / nine) cousins.
3. Dave is (a grandfather / a father / an uncle).
4. Matt has (two cousins and one sister / three aunts or uncles / a small family).
5. Matt's house is (noisy / quiet / crazy).

B Complete the sentences so they are true for you.

1. I think big families are _____ .
2. I think small families are _____ .
3. I have _____ brothers and / or sisters. I think _____ .
4. I have _____ aunts and / or uncles. I think _____ .

Your turn

Write

A Complete the web.

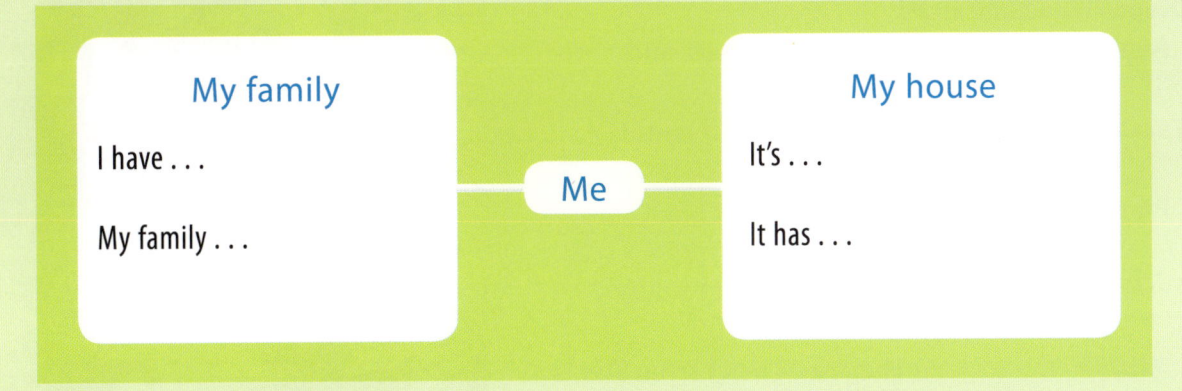

My family
I have . . .
My family . . .

Me

My house
It's . . .
It has . . .

B Write about your family and your house. Use the web in Part A to help you.

I have _____

Family and Home 69

UNIT 5 Review

Language chart review

has / have statements	We're / They're; Our / Their	What's . . . like?
I **have** two sisters. I **have** no brothers. He **has** a big family. She **has** an apartment. It **has** one bedroom.	**We're** from New York. **Our** last name is Diaz. **They're** from Chicago. **Their** last name is Carlton. We're = We are They're = They are	**What's** she **like**? She's **nice**.

A Complete the conversation.

Farah This is a picture of ___our___ (we / our) family.
Diego You and Paul _____ (have / has) a big family.
Farah Yeah. We _____ (have / has) a lot of brothers and sisters.
Diego Who's this?
Paul This is _____ (we / our) brother, Kyle.
Diego What's he like?
Paul _____ (He's / His) smart and a little shy.
Farah This is _____ (we / our) aunt, Carmen, and uncle, Larry.
Paul _____ (They're / Their) last name is Parsons.
Farah _____ (They're / Their) really friendly and nice.
Paul _____ (They're / Their) from Texas.
Diego I'm from Arizona.
Farah _____ (We're / Our) from Arizona, too!

B Read the conversation again. Answer these questions.

1. What's their brother like? _____
2. What are their aunt and uncle like? _____
3. Where is their uncle from? _____
4. Where are Farah and Paul from? _____

C Complete the sentences with the words in the box.

☐ her   ☐ his   ☑ my   ☐ my   ☐ our   ☐ their   ☐ your

I'm Johnny Martin. This is ___my___ father. _____ name is Cal. _____ mother's name is Kimberly. I have one sister. _____ name is Nicki. I have two brothers, too. _____ names are Darren and Leo. _____ family is pretty big. What's _____ family like?

D Write about your family. Use some of the words from Part C.

I'm . . . _____

_____

_____

E What's the difference? Compare Amy's house and Ben's house. Write sentences with *has* and *has no*.

Amy's house

Ben's house

1. (bedroom) _Amy's house has three bedrooms._
   Ben's house has two bedrooms.

2. (living room) _____

3. (bathroom) _____

4. (dining room) _____

5. (kitchen) _____

6. (garage) _____

Time for the Theme Project? See page 130.

Family and Home 71

Lesson 21: The media center

1. Vocabulary

A Look at the picture of the new media center and write the names of the items. Use the words in the box. Then listen and practice.

T.100

- ☑ board
- ☐ cabinet
- ☐ printer
- ☐ scanner
- ☐ bookcase
- ☐ CD/DVD player
- ☐ remote control
- ☐ screen

1. _____
2. _____
3. _____
4. _____
5. _____
6. _____
7. _____
8. _____

B Ask and answer questions about things in your classroom.

What's that?   It's a board.   What are those?   They're computers.

UNIT 6 At School

2. Language focus

A There is a problem in the media center.
Listen and practice.

> *There's / There are . . .*
> **There's a** printer.
> **There are** six computers.
>
> *There's no / There are no . . .*
> **There's no** wastebasket.
> **There are no** chairs.
>
> There's = There is

Mr. Wilson   So, here's the new media center.
Ms. Brooks   Wow! It's great.
Mr. Wilson   Wait a minute . . .
             There's a problem.
Ms. Brooks   What's wrong?
Mr. Wilson   Well, there are only six computers.
Ms. Brooks   Oh, dear. Well, there's a printer.
             Is that right?
Mr. Wilson   Yes, that's OK. But there's no
             wastebasket, and there are no chairs.
Ms. Brooks   Oh, no!

Mr. Wilson
Clarkston Middle School

- ☐ 2 boards
- ☐ 2 bookcases
- ☐ 2 cabinets
- ☐ 1 remote control
- ☐ 1 CD/DVD player
- ☐ 8 chairs
- ☑ 8 computers
- ☐ 8 desks
- ☑ 1 printer
- ☐ 1 screen
- ☐ 1 scanner
- ☐ 1 wastebasket

B Look at Mr. Wilson's order form in Exercise 2A. Then look at the picture on page 72.
What's right? What's wrong? Write sentences. Then listen and check.

What's right?	What's wrong?
There's a printer.	*There are six computers.*

3. Speaking

Make true or false statements about your classroom. Your classmate says
Yes or *No* and corrects the false statements.

You   There's a board.
Classmate Yes.
You   There are 12 chairs.
Classmate No. There are 20 chairs.

At School   73

Lesson 22 — Around school

1. Vocabulary

A Label the photos of Jenny's school with the words in the brochure. Then listen and practice.

Kent International School Has A Lot!

1. gym
2.
3.
4.
5.
6.
7.
8.
9.

Sports Facilities
- 2 tennis courts
- 4 athletic fields
  * 1 football field
  * 1 baseball field
  * 2 soccer fields
- gym
- swimming pool

Media Center
- computer lab with 50 computers
- language lab

Other Facilities
- auditorium
- library
- cafeteria

B Write about the facilities at your school. Use *There is / There are*.

There is . . .

2. Language focus

A Jenny's cousin, Jill, asks about Kent International School. Listen and practice.

T.104

Jill	Jenny, your school is really great. Are there any tennis courts?
Jenny	Yes, there are. There's a tennis team, too.
Jill	So, are there any cute players?
Jenny	No, there aren't.
Jill	Hmm. Is there a soccer team?
Jenny	Yes, there is.
Jill	Is there a game today?
Jenny	No, there isn't. Sorry.

> **Is there a / Are there any . . . ?**
>
> **Is there a** soccer team?
>   Yes, **there is**.
>   No, **there isn't**.
>
> **Are there any** tennis courts?
>   Yes, **there are**.
>   No, **there aren't**.
>
> isn't = is not   aren't = are not

B Complete the rest of the conversation. Listen and check. Then practice.

T.105

Jill   __Are__ there any other interesting things at your school?
Jenny   Yes, there _____ . There are some new classrooms and a new media center.
Jill   Oh, that's cool. _____ there an Internet café there?
Jenny   No, there _____ .
Jill   Hey, I'm hungry. Are there _____ cafés near here?
Jenny   No, there _____ . But there's a cafeteria.
Jill   Are _____ any cute boys there?
Jenny   Yes, there _____ . Let's go!

3. Pronunciation *th*

A Listen to the two pronunciations of *th*. Then listen again and practice.

T.106

Voiced			Unvoiced		
there	**th**at	fa**th**er	**th**ree	**th**ink	ba**th**room

B Write these words in the correct columns: *birthday, brother, mother, thanks, the, they, thing, thirty*. Listen and check. Then practice.

T.107

Voiced	Unvoiced

At School 75

Lessons 21 & 22 Mini-review

1. Language check

A Read about the neighborhood around Kent International School. Then answer the questions.

Enjoy your free time after school!

Bob's Burgers
Hamburgers, sandwiches, and more!
325 Main Street
555-0982

Kent Shopping Mall
48 stores,
5 movie theaters
25 Park Avenue
555-1618

Central Park
56th–60th Streets
Swimming pool
Soccer and baseball fields

Lee's Restaurant
Great Chinese food!
16 West Avenue
555-6723

City Video Arcade
Your place for after-school fun!
18 South Avenue
555-8722

Maple Bookstore and Internet Café
New and used books
Kent Shopping Mall
555-8655

1. Are there any stores near the school? *Yes, there are.*
2. Are there any athletic fields in the neighborhood? _____
3. Is there a basketball court in the park? _____
4. Is there a bookstore at the mall? _____
5. Are there any restaurants on South Avenue? _____
6. Is there a video arcade in the neighborhood? _____

B Write three sentences about your neighborhood. Then tell your classmates.

There's a park.

1. _____
2. _____
3. _____

There's a park. There . . .

76 Unit 6

C Look at the picture. Circle the correct words to complete the sentences.

1. There's a (cabinet /(wastebasket)) next to the desk.
2. There's a large (computer / board) on the desk.
3. There's a (scanner / CD/DVD player) under the desk.
4. There's a (remote control / screen) next to the CD/DVD player.
5. There are no (chairs / pencils) near the desk.
6. There's a (bookcase / printer) next to the computer.

2. Listening

People talk about their schools. Listen and answer the questions.
T.108 Write the correct information for *No* answers.

1. Are there two scanners in the media center? *No, there aren't. There's one scanner.*
2. Are the answers on the screen? _____
3. Are there five wastebaskets in the classroom? _____
4. Is there a football field at Jim's school? _____
5. Are there three swimming pools at Mia's school? _____
6. Are there 20 computers in the computer lab? _____

Time for a Game?
See page 119.

At School 77

Lesson 23: School subjects

1. Vocabulary

A These are some of the classes at Kent International School. Label the books with the words in the box. Then listen and practice.

- ☐ art
- ☐ geography
- ☐ history
- ☐ music
- ☐ science
- ☐ English
- ☐ health
- ☐ math
- ☑ physical education (P.E.)
- ☐ Spanish

1. P.E.
2.
3.
4.
5.
6.
7.
8.
9.
10.

B Make a list of your school subjects. Are they easy or difficult for you? Check (✓) *Easy* or *Difficult*. Then tell your classmates.

My school subjects	Easy	Difficult
_____	☐	☐
_____	☐	☐
_____	☐	☐
_____	☐	☐
_____	☐	☐

My school subjects	Easy	Difficult
_____	☐	☐
_____	☐	☐
_____	☐	☐
_____	☐	☐
_____	☐	☐

I think geography is *easy*.

I think math is *difficult*.

2. Saying the time

🎧 **Look at the days and times in Nicole's class schedule. Listen and practice.**
T.110

Saying the time
8:30 = eight thirty
1:05 = one-oh-five
2:00 = two *or* two o'clock

Class Schedule for Nicole Martel

	Monday	Tuesday	Wednesday	Thursday	Friday
8:30	English	English	English	English	English
9:25	math	math	math	computer lab	math
10:20	P.E.	health	P.E.	art	P.E.
11:15	lunch	lunch	lunch	lunch	lunch
12:10	history	geography	history	geography	history
1:05	science	science	science lab	science	science
2:00	Spanish	language lab	Spanish	music	Spanish

3. Language focus

on / at
I have computer lab **on** Thursday.
My computer lab is **at** 9:25.

🎧 **A Nicole talks about her class schedule. Listen and practice.**
T.111

> This is my school schedule. I have English class every day at 8:30. I think English is easy.
>
> I have history class at 12:10 on Monday, Wednesday, and Friday. History is difficult.
>
> My favorite day is Thursday. I have computer lab at 9:25. It's great!

🎧 **B Look at Nicole's class schedule in Exercise 2 above. Complete the sentences with the day and time. Then listen and check.**
T.112

1. Nicole's health class is *on Tuesday at 10:20* .
2. Nicole has science lab _____ .
3. Her geography class is _____ .
4. She has Spanish class _____ .
5. Her language lab is _____ .

4. Speaking

What are your three favorite classes at school? When are they? Tell your classmates.

> I think math is great. I have math class on Tuesday at 1:00. I think . . .

At School **79**

Lesson 24 Spring Day

1. Vocabulary

A Look at the Spring Day poster. Listen and practice.

Kent International School
Spring Day — Food, fun, games, and more!

- **Spelling Contest** 9:00 a.m. / **nine o'clock**
- **Fashion Show** 10:15 a.m. / **a quarter after ten**
- **Bicycle Race** 11:20 a.m. / **twenty after eleven**
- **Picnic** 12:00 p.m. / **noon**
- **Band Concert** 1:45 p.m. / **a quarter to two**
- **Soccer Game** 3:30 p.m. / **half past three**

B What time are the events? Complete the sentences.

1. The _____ is at a quarter after ten.
2. The picnic is at _____ .
3. The soccer game is at _____ .

2. Language focus

A Yoshi and Paulo are at Spring Day. Listen and practice.

Yoshi Are you excited about Spring Day?
Paulo Yes, I am. I'm in the spelling contest and the soccer game.
Yoshi Uh, what time is the spelling contest?
Paulo It's at nine o'clock. What time is it now?
Yoshi It's five minutes after nine.
Paulo Oh, no! I'm already late.

> **What time . . . ?**
> **What time** is it now?
>   It's 9:05. (It's nine-oh-five.)
>   It's five (minutes) after nine.
> **What time** is the spelling contest?
>   It's at nine (o'clock).

B It's Spring Day at another International School. Write questions and answers. Then listen and check.

1. (bicycle race) _What time is the bicycle race?_
   (10:15) _It's at a quarter after ten._

2. (fashion show) _____
   (3:30) _____

3. (band concert) _____
   (12:20) _____

4. (picnic) _____
   (1:15) _____

5. (soccer game) _____
   (2:45) _____

3. Listening

What time is it now? Listen and check (✓) the correct time.

1. ✓ [clock]
2. ☐ 1:45
3. ☐ [clock]
4. ☐ 3:45
5. ☐ [clock]

☐ [clock]
☐ 1:30
☐ [clock]
☐ 3:30
☐ [clock]

At School 81

UNIT 6 Get Connected

Read

A Read the information quickly. Check (✓) the times you find.

☐ 12:30   ☐ 3:30   ☐ 9:15
☐ 9:00   ☐ 3:15   ☐ 12:30

Welcome to Fun & Art!

Every **summer**, kids (ages 7–16) from around the world go to Fun & Art in Denton, Texas. At Fun & Art, there are cool classes in **3D animation, fashion design, cooking** – and a lot of other classes, too. Is Fun & Art a school? No, it's a **summer camp**!

What time are classes every day? Well, students have their first class at 9:00 a.m., and they have lunch at 12:30 p.m. They have other classes at 3:15 p.m. – soccer, basketball, **juggling** . . . At 7:00 p.m., students go to the movies, go bowling, play games, have talent shows . . . It's everybody's favorite time of day.

Are there any classrooms at Fun & Art? Yes, there are, and there are also computer labs, a gym, a swimming pool, and sports fields. Fun & Art has a lot of things. It's great!

B 🎧 T.117 Read the article slowly. Check your answers in Part A.

More Vocabulary Practice? See page 124.

C Answer the questions.

1. Are there cool classes at Fun & Art? *Yes, there are.*
2. Is Fun & Art a summer camp? _____
3. What time is the first class every day? _____
4. What time is lunch? _____
5. Are there computer labs and sports fields at Fun & Art? _____

What time is the game?

Listen

A 🎧 T.118 Elsa and Chris talk about summer camp. Listen and write *True* or *False*. Then correct the false statements.

1. Chris is excited about summer camp. *False.*   *Chris isn't excited about summer camp.*
2. Chris has science class at 10:00. _____   _____
3. Chris has P.E. at summer camp. _____   _____
4. There's a gym at Chris's summer camp. _____   _____
5. The basketball game is at 3:30 on Saturday. _____   _____
6. The picnic is at noon on Saturday. _____   _____

B Complete the statements so they are true for you.

1. I think summer camp is _____ .
2. I think math and English classes in the summer are _____ .
3. I think basketball is _____ .
4. I think picnics with friends are _____ .

Your turn

Write

A Think about your dream summer camp. Answer the questions about it.

1. What's the name of your summer camp? _____
2. Where is it? _____
3. What's at the camp? A swimming pool? A sports field? A computer lab?
   _____
4. What's the schedule every day? _____

B Write about your dream summer camp. Use the answers in Part A to help you.

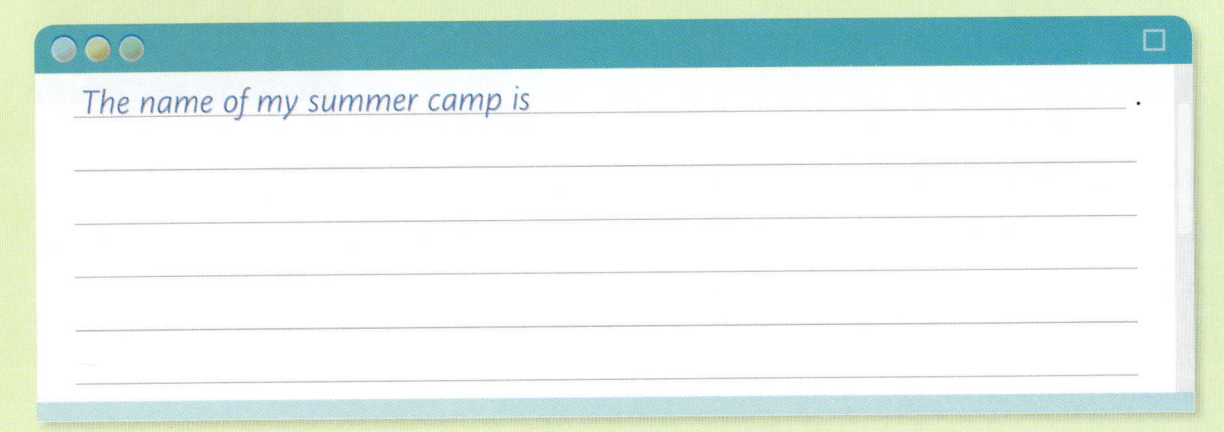

The name of my summer camp is _____ .

At School 83

UNIT 6 Review

Language chart review

There's / There are
There's a nice library in my neighborhood.   **There's no** library in my neighborhood.
There are two athletic fields at my school.   **There are no** athletic fields at my school.

Is there a / Are there any . . . ?
Is there a park in your neighborhood?   **Are there any** restaurants in your neighborhood?
Yes, **there is**.   Yes, **there are**.
No, **there isn't**.   No, **there aren't**.

There's = There is   isn't = is not   aren't = are not

A Complete the e-mails with *there's, there are, there's no,* and *there are no.*

From: Claudia
Hi, Terri!
Here's a picture of my city – Rio de Janeiro, Brazil. *There are* many interesting places here. Rio has a lot of beaches. My favorite beach is Copacabana Beach. _____ a famous mountain here, too. It's Sugar Loaf. _____ a theater downtown. It's the Municipal Theater. _____ many concerts at the theater. The National Museum of Fine Arts is famous. It's a great city. I love it!
Come visit me soon!
Claudia

From: Terri
Dear Claudia,
Thanks for your e-mail. Rio is beautiful. My town is very small. _____ museum here. _____ beaches here. _____ a theater. _____ two restaurants and an Internet café. My town is a little boring, but I like it a lot!
Bye!
Terri

B Write questions and answers about Terri's town.

1. (a museum) **Q:** *Is there a museum?*   **A:** *No, there isn't.*
2. (a café) **Q:** _____ **A:** _____
3. (any beaches) **Q:** _____ **A:** _____
4. (any restaurants) **Q:** _____ **A:** _____

Language chart review

What time . . . ?	on / at

What time is it?
    It's ten forty-five.
What time is the concert?
    It's at six.
	I have art **on** Tuesday.
	Lunch is **at** 11:15.
	There's a soccer game **on** Monday **at** 5:00.

C Write questions to complete the conversation.

Sandra *Is there a volleyball game tonight?*

Tyler Yes, there is. There's a volleyball game in the gym.

Sandra _____ ?

Tyler It's at 10:00.

Sandra _____ ?

Tyler Hmm . . . It's 9:45, now.

Sandra Let's hurry!

D Look at the posters and write sentences.

CONCERT — Tuesday 8:00 p.m.

VOLLEYBALL GAME — Thursday 1:00 p.m.

1. *There's a concert on Tuesday at eight o'clock.*
2. _____

Birthday PARTY — Friday 7:30 p.m.

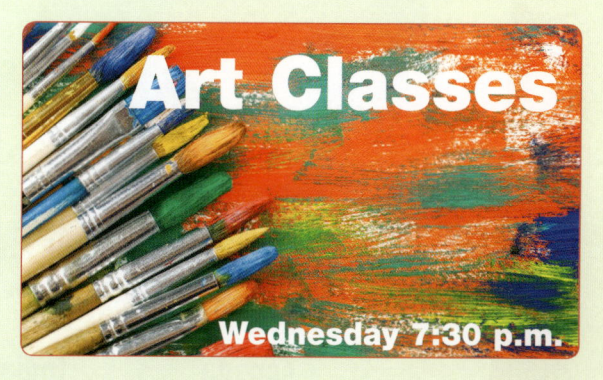

Art Classes — Wednesday 7:30 p.m.

3. _____
4. _____

Time fo the Theme Project?
See page 131.

At School **85**

Lesson 25: People and countries

1. Vocabulary

A English is an official language in over 50 countries. Here are some of the countries. Listen and practice.
(T.119)

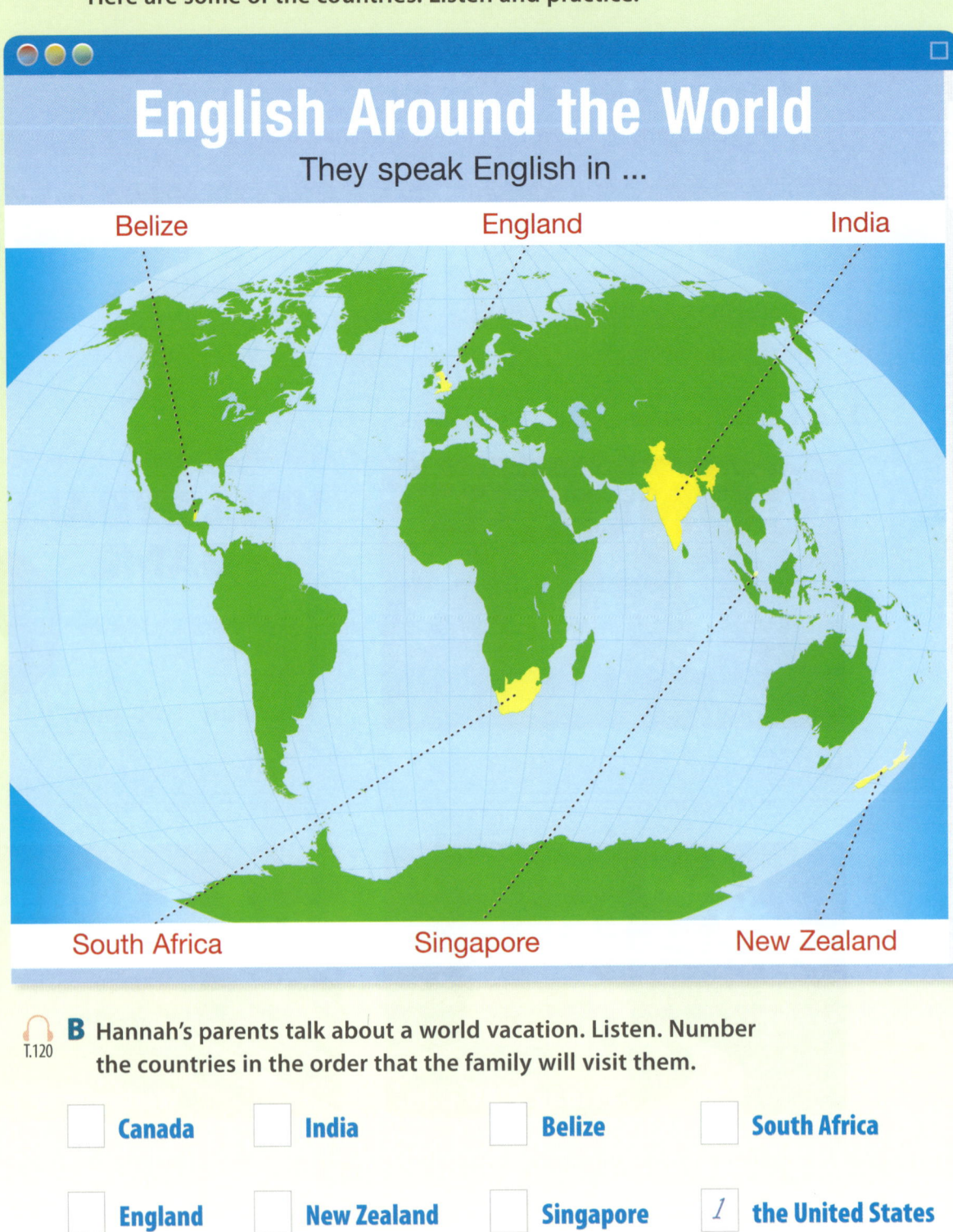

English Around the World
They speak English in ...

- Belize
- England
- India
- South Africa
- Singapore
- New Zealand

B Hannah's parents talk about a world vacation. Listen. Number the countries in the order that the family will visit them.
(T.120)

- ☐ Canada
- ☐ India
- ☐ Belize
- ☐ South Africa
- ☐ England
- ☐ New Zealand
- ☐ Singapore
- ☐ 1 the United States

2. Language focus

A Hannah shows her vacation photos to Mark. Listen and practice.

is / isn't; are / aren't in short answers	
Is she from India?	Yes, she **is**.
Is he from Singapore?	No, he **isn't**.
Are they from Singapore?	Yes, they **are**.
Are they from New Zealand?	No, they **aren't**.

isn't = is not   aren't = are not

Hannah Here I am with Tom and Bruce.
Mark Are they from England?
Hannah No, they aren't. They're from New Zealand.
Mark Wow! Look at this photo. These girls are very pretty! Are they from Singapore?
Hannah Yes, they are. I have their e-mails. I can introduce you.
Mark Great! And this boy? Is he from Singapore, too?
Hannah No, he isn't. He's from India. His name is Ravi. And this is his friend, Usha.
Mark Is she from India, too?
Hannah Yes, she is.
Mark Wow! You have a lot of new friends!
Hannah Yes, and they all speak English!

B Look at Part A. Answer the questions. Then listen and check.

1. Are Tom and Bruce from Canada?   *No, they aren't.*
2. Is Ravi from India?   _____
3. Is Usha from Singapore?   _____
4. Are the girls from England?   _____
5. Are the girls from Singapore?   _____

3. Speaking

Complete the sentences with names of places.
A classmate guesses the places.

He's from New Zealand.

He's from _____ .

She's from _____ .

They're from _____ .

Classmate Is he from Belize?
You No, he isn't.
Classmate Is he from New Zealand?
You Yes, he is.

Around the World

Lesson 26 — Nationalities

1. Vocabulary

A Take the Internet quiz. Match the photos to the correct texts. Then listen and practice. *(T.123)*

International Stars Quiz

Who are these stars? Take the quiz and see what you know.

1. Alessandra Ambrosio
2. Hiroki Kuroda
3. Vitor Faverani
4. Emma Watson

- [ ] He's on an **American** basketball team, but he's from Brazil.
- [ ] He's a famous **Japanese** baseball player. Baseball is popular in Japan.
- [ ] She's a **British** actor. I think she's great!
- [1] This model is **Brazilian**. She's really pretty.

B Complete the chart with the words in the box. Then listen and practice. *(T.124)*

- ✓ American
- ☐ Brazilian
- ☐ Canadian
- ☐ Japanese
- ☐ Peruvian
- ☐ South Korean
- ☐ Australian
- ☐ British
- ☐ French
- ☐ Mexican
- ☐ Puerto Rican
- ☐ Spanish

Place	Nationality
1. the United States	American
2. Japan	
3. Brazil	
4. Spain	
5. England	
6. France	

Place	Nationality
7. South Korea	
8. Australia	
9. Puerto Rico	
10. Peru	
11. Mexico	
12. Canada	

2. Pronunciation Syllable stress

🎧 T.125 Listen. Underline the stressed part of each word. Then listen again and practice.

1. Ca <u>na</u> di an
2. <u>Mex</u> i can
3. Ko re an
4. Pe ru vi an
5. Bri tish
6. Jap a nese
7. A mer i can
8. Span ish
9. Puer to Ri can
10. Bra zil ian
11. Aus tral ian
12. Co lom bi an

3. Language focus

🎧 T.126 Complete the quiz with *isn't* or *aren't*. Who are these stars? Listen and check.

> **isn't / aren't in statements**
> He **isn't** American.
> His movies **aren't** all in English.

International Stars Quiz

5 This actor is famous in the U.S., but he isn't American. He's Mexican. His movies aren't all in English. Some of his movies are in Spanish. His movies usually aren't funny. They're serious. Who is he?

6 This star _____ Peruvian. She's American, and her parents are from Puerto Rico. She's a singer and an actor. A lot of her movies _____ serious. They're funny. Her fans _____ all from the U.S. They're from around the world! Who is she?

4. Speaking

Make false statements about stars to a classmate. Your classmate corrects them.

You Vitor Faverani is British.
Classmate He isn't British. He's Brazilian.

Around the World **89**

Lessons 25 & 26 Mini-review

1. Language check

A Number the sentences in the correct order.

___ **Jake** No, they aren't. They're from Peru. But their mother – my aunt – isn't Peruvian.

_1_ **Jake** Look at this picture of my cousins.

___ **Luisa** Yeah. But my father and I aren't Japanese. We're Canadian.

___ **Jake** And I'm Canadian, too!

___ **Luisa** Are they from Canada?

___ **Luisa** Really? Is she Colombian?

___ **Jake** Wow! That's interesting.

___ **Luisa** Really? My mother is Japanese.

___ **Jake** No, she isn't. She's Japanese.

B Look at Part A. Answer the questions.

1. Are Jake's cousins from Peru?

   Yes, they are.

2. Is Jake's aunt Canadian?

   _____

3. Is Luisa's mother Japanese?

   _____

4. Are Luisa and her father Japanese?

   _____

5. Is Jake Canadian?

   _____

C Look at Jenny's e-mail address book. Then correct the sentences below.

Full name	City / Place	E-mail addre
Amanda Dart	Sydney, Australia	adat@prestl
Mike Maynard	Montreal, Canada	mmaynard@
Emiko Koga	Kyoto, Japan	Koga@iscolr
Jack Crowe	Melbourne, Australia	jackc@prisrg
Juan Rivera	Acapulco, Mexico	jrivera@yallo
Peter Stockwell	Vancouver, Canada	Pstock3@co
Claudia Ferreira	São Paulo, Brazil	claferr@spet

1. Emiko is Canadian. *She isn't Canadian. She's Japanese.*
2. Melbourne and Sydney are in Japan. *They aren't . . .*
3. Claudia is from Mexico.
4. Juan and Amanda are from Canada.
5. Peter is American.
6. Kyoto is in Brazil.
7. Montreal and Vancouver are in the United States.

D Now check your answers with a classmate.

— Is Emiko Canadian?
— No, she isn't. She's Japanese.

2. Listening

A Paulo talks about his e-pals. Listen and check (✓) their nationalities.

1. Lee	☐ South Korean	☐ Puerto Rican
2. Ashley and Helen	☐ Australian	☐ British
3. Alberto	☐ Peruvian	☐ Mexican
4. Angela and Hector	☐ American	☐ Spanish

B Compare answers with a classmate.

— Lee is . . . .
— That's right.

Time for a Game? See page 120.

Lesson 27: Holidays

1. Vocabulary

A Listen and practice the months of the year.

> January February March April May June July
> August September October November December

B When are these holidays in the U.S.? Complete the sentences with the months below. Then listen and practice.

☐ February   ☑ May   ☐ June   ☐ July   ☐ November   ☐ December

1. Mother's Day is in _May_.
2. Thanksgiving is in _____. 
3. Valentine's Day is in _____. 
4. Father's Day is in _____. 
5. Independence Day is in _____. 
6. New Year's Eve is in _____. 

C Talk about your favorite holiday with a classmate.

You What's your favorite holiday?
Classmate It's .... It's in .... What's your favorite holiday?
You It's .... It's in ....

92 Unit 7

2. Language focus

A Jenny chats with her e-pal, José. Listen and practice.

T.130

> **When is . . . ?**
> **When is** Independence Day?
> It's **in July**.

José: Jenny, are you online?
Jenny: Yes, I am. How are you, José?
José: I'm great. It's Independence Day in Mexico today. It's a holiday – no school. Yay!
Jenny: Wow, you're lucky. I'm at school right now.
José: When is Independence Day in the U.S.?
Jenny: It's in July. It's my favorite holiday.

B Look at Exercise 1B. Write four questions about holidays in the U.S. Then ask and answer the questions.

When is New Year's Eve?

1. _____
2. _____
3. _____
4. _____

— When is New Year's Eve?
— It's in December.

3. Listening

A When are these holidays? Listen and match the two parts of each sentence.

T.131

1. Independence Day in Mexico is in ____
2. Thanksgiving Day in Canada is in ____
3. Children's Day in Japan is in ____
4. Australia Day is in ____

a. January.
b. May.
c. September.
d. October.

B Ask and answer questions about holidays in your country.

— When is Carnaval in Brazil?
— It's in February or March.

Around the World

Lesson 28: Important days

1. Vocabulary

A Look at the calendar. Listen and practice the numbers.

March

Sunday	Monday	Tuesday	Wednesday	Thursday	Friday	Saturday
1st first	2nd second	3rd third	4th fourth	5th fifth	6th sixth	7th seventh
8th eighth	9th ninth	10th tenth	11th eleventh	12th twelfth	13th thirteenth	14th fourteenth
15th fifteenth	16th sixteenth	17th seventeenth	18th eighteenth	19th nineteenth	20th twentieth	21st twenty-first
22nd twenty-second	23rd twenty-third	24th twenty-fourth	25th twenty-fifth	26th twenty-sixth	27th twenty-seventh	28th twenty-eighth
29th twenty-ninth	30th thirtieth	31st thirty-first				

B Say these dates. Then listen and practice.

January 1st   April 5th   July 3rd   October 31st
February 22nd   May 17th   August 12th   November 18th
March 13th   June 11th   September 9th   December 24th

2. Listening

Paulo and Nicole make a list of birthdays. Listen and complete the chart.

Name	Birthday
Sandra	September twelfth
Jenny	
Tyler	
Yoshi	
Nicole	
Paulo	

Unit 7

3. Language focus

A Daryl and Kimberly are e-pals. They write about their favorite months. Listen and practice.

in / on
The first day of school is **in September**.
My best friend's birthday is **on September 28th**.

The first day of school is in September. And my best friend's birthday is on September 28th. He has great parties. I'm always happy in September.

Daryl
Dallas, U.S.

My favorite month is December. The last day of school is on December 22nd. My birthday is on December 31st. There are a lot of holidays in December, too.

Kimberly
Auckland, New Zealand

B Complete the sentences with *in* or *on*. For items 5 and 6, use your own information. Then listen and check.

1. There are a lot of holidays ___in___ November.
2. Valentine's Day is _____ February 14th.
3. Father's Day is _____ June.
4. Independence Day in the U.S. is _____ July 4th.
5. My last day of school is _____.
6. My best friend's birthday is _____.

4. Speaking

Ask four classmates about their birthdays. Then complete the chart.

You When's your birthday?
Classmate It's on . . . .

Classmate	Birthday

Around the World 95

UNIT 7 Get Connected

Read

A Read the article quickly. Check (✓) the statements that are true.

☐ 1. It's everyone's birthday on the first day of the New Year's celebration in Thailand.
☐ 2. Children throw water out the window on New Year's Eve in Puerto Rico.
☐ 3. The famous New Year's ball goes down in Times Square on New Year's Eve.

New Year's Fun Around the World

The New Year's holiday is **important** around the world. There are some interesting **celebrations**, but they aren't only on January 1.

In Vietnam, the New Year's celebration is in February and everyone's birthday is on the first day of that celebration! Children **receive** money from their families and good friends. The money is very lucky.

In Thailand, the New Year's celebration is on April 15. Everyone **throws water** on their friends for good luck. Puerto Rican children throw water, too. They throw it out the **window** at 12:00 a.m. on New Year's Eve (December 31). It's really fun – and lucky!

On New Year's Eve, a lot of people in the U.S. watch the famous New Year's ball go down in Times Square in New York City. It's really cool! When is the New Year's holiday in your country?

B 🎧 T.137 Read the article slowly. Check your answers in Part A.

More Vocabulary Practice? See page 125.

C Answer the questions.

1. When is everyone's birthday in Vietnam? *Everyone's birthday is in February.*
2. What's lucky for children in Vietnam to receive on New Year's? _____
3. When is the New Year's celebration in Thailand? _____
4. In Puerto Rico, when is it lucky to throw water out the window? _____
5. Where's the famous New Year's ball in the U.S.? _____

It's in January or February.

Listen

A 🎧 T.138 Andy and Kim talk about holidays. Listen and answer the questions.

1. Is Ming Chinese? Yes, he is.
2. When is Chinese New Year? _____
3. Is Ming excited? _____
4. What's Kim's favorite day? _____
5. What time is the party? _____

B Complete the sentences so they are true for you.

1. I think New Year's Day is _____ in my country.
2. I think Valentine's Day is _____ .
3. Birthday parties are _____ .
4. Holidays with families and friends are _____ .

Your turn

Write

A Complete the chart about holidays in your country.

	When is it?	What's the holiday like?
What's an important holiday?		
What's your favorite holiday?		
What's a boring holiday?		

B Write about the three holidays. Use the chart in Part A to help you.

_____ is a very important holiday in my country.
It's on / in _____ .
_____
_____

Around the World 97

UNIT 7 Review

Language chart review

isn't / aren't in statements	isn't / aren't in short answers	Questions with *when* in / on
She **isn't** American. They **aren't** French.	**Is she** American? Yes, **she is**. No, **she isn't**. **Are they** Peruvian? Yes, **they are**. No, **they aren't**.	**When is** Bobby's birthday? It's **in** June. It's **on** June 2nd.

A Read the article. Then answer the questions.

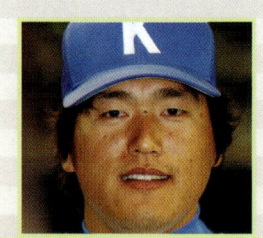

Hee-Seop Choi – baseball player
Country: South Korea
Birthday: March 16, 1979
First American team: The Chicago Cubs (2003)

Shakira – singer
Country: Colombia
Birthday: February 2, 1977
First album: *Magia* (1991)

Wagner Moura – actor
Country: Brazil
Birthday: June 27, 1976
First movie: *Woman on Top (2000)*

Marion Cotillard – actor
Country: France
Birthday: September 30, 1975
First awards: The Golden Globe and the Academy Award (2008)

Abigail Breslin – actor
Country: United States
Birthday: April 14, 1996
First movie: *Signs* (2002)

1. Is Shakira from Brazil? *No, she isn't.*
2. Is Hee-Seop a soccer player? _____
3. Are Abigail and Marion actors? _____
4. Is Wagner Brazilian? _____
5. Are Shakira and Marion's birthdays in August? _____
6. Is Wagner's birthday in June? _____

98 Unit 7

B Look at Part A. Write about two people.

   Shakira is a singer. She's Colombian.
   Her birthday is on February 2nd.

1. _____

2. _____

C Look at Pauline's calendar. Write a question for each answer.

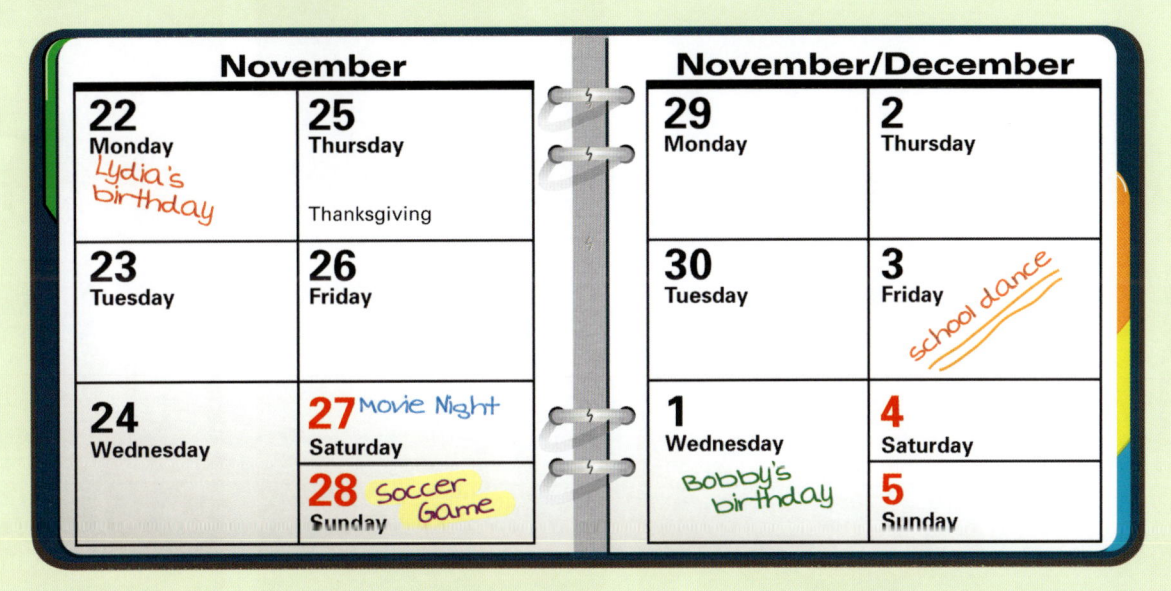

November

22 Monday — Lydia's birthday	25 Thursday — Thanksgiving
23 Tuesday	26 Friday
24 Wednesday	27 Saturday — Movie Night / 28 Sunday — Soccer Game

November/December

29 Monday	2 Thursday
30 Tuesday	3 Friday — school dance
1 Wednesday — Bobby's birthday	4 Saturday / 5 Sunday

1. Q: When is the school dance? A: It's on December 3rd.
2. Q: _____ A: It's on November 25th.
3. Q: _____ A: It's on November 27th.
4. Q: _____ A: It's on December 1st.

D Look at Pauline's calendar again. Correct the sentences with *isn't* and *aren't*. Spell out the numbers.

1. Lydia's birthday is on November 23rd. Lydia's birthday isn't on November twenty-third. It's on November twenty-second.

2. The soccer game and movie night are in December. _____

3. Movie night is November 28th. _____

4. The school dance is on December 1st. _____

5. Bobby's birthday is in November. _____

Time for the Theme Project
See page 132.

Around the World

Lesson 29 — Favorite places

1. Vocabulary

A These are three students' favorite places. Match the photos to the correct texts. Then listen and practice.

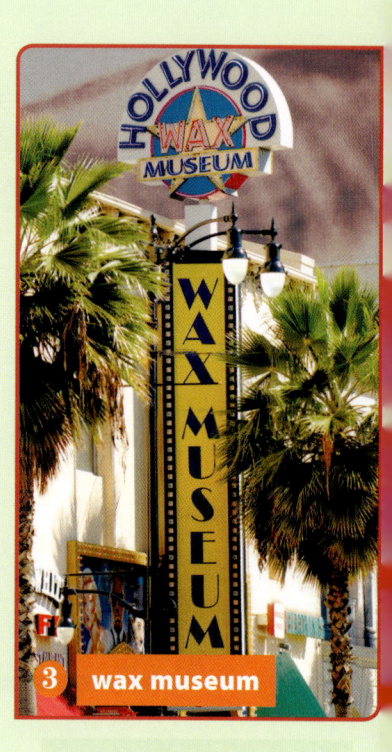

T.139

1. beach
2. zoo
3. wax museum

☐ This place is in Singapore. It's *interesting*. It's not *boring*. There are animals from around the world here. There are kangaroos from Australia in this place.

☐ This place is in Los Angeles. It's *fun*, but it's always *busy*. There are wax models of famous actors. There's even a model of Angelina Jolie.

☐ This place is in Mazatlán, Mexico. It's *beautiful*. It's really *exciting*, too. It's my favorite place for a vacation.

B Read the words. What places do you think of? Complete the chart and then tell your classmates.

Word	Place
beautiful	*Ipanema Beach*
boring	
exciting	

Word	Place
interesting	
busy	
fun	

Ipanema Beach is beautiful.

UNIT 8 Teen Time

100

2. Language focus

What's it like?
What's it like?
It's fun.

A Tyler and Yoshi talk about their favorite places. Listen and practice.

T.140

Tyler What's your favorite place in Tokyo, Yoshi?
Yoshi It's Odaiba.
Tyler What's it like?
Yoshi It's fun. There are a lot of things there. There are beaches, parks, stores, and museums. Joypolis Park is also there.
Tyler What's it like?
Yoshi It's great. It has a lot of video games.

B Complete the conversation. Listen and check. Then practice.

T.141

Tyler I like New York a lot.
Yoshi _____
Tyler It's big and exciting. I like the Empire State Building, too.
Yoshi _____
Tyler It's really beautiful. And there's an observatory on the 102nd floor.

C Ask a classmate about a favorite place in your town or city.

A What's your favorite place in . . . . . . ?
B It's . . . .
A What's it like?
B It's . . . .

3. Listening

T.142

Jenny, Paulo, and Sandra talk to Tyler about a museum. What's it like? Listen and check (✓) the correct words.

	Beautiful	Interesting	Exciting	Fun	Busy	Boring
Jenny	✓	☐	✓	☐	☐	☐
Paulo	☐	☐	☐	☐	☐	☐
Sandra	☐	☐	☐	☐	☐	☐

Lesson 30 — Talent show

1. Vocabulary

A There is a talent show at Kent International School. Look at the bulletin board. Label the photos with the words in the box. Then listen and practice.

- ☐ dance
- ☑ play Ping-Pong
- ☐ sing
- ☐ draw
- ☐ play the guitar
- ☐ skateboard

Enter the Talent Show!

1. play Ping-Pong
2.
3.
4.
5.
6.

B Who in your class can enter the talent show? Write one name for each category.

Category	Name
dance	
play the guitar	
draw	

Category	Name
sing	
play Ping-Pong	
skateboard	

102   Unit 8

2. Language focus

A Paulo and Sandra talk about the talent show. Listen and practice.

T.144

Paulo Look! There's a talent show on Sunday. Let's enter.
Sandra Um . . . no, thanks.
Paulo Oh, come on. I can play the guitar. I can't sing. Can you sing?
Sandra No, I can't. I can't sing at all.
Paulo Can you dance?
Sandra Yes, I can. But . . .
Paulo So, let's enter the show.
Sandra You and me? You're kidding! I'm too shy.

can / can't

I **can** dance. She **can't** sing.
Can you dance? **Can** she sing?
Yes, I **can**. No, she **can't**.

Use *can* for all subjects:
 I, you, he, she, we, they

B Write two things Paulo and Sandra can and can't do. Then listen and check.

T.145

1. Paulo _____ .
2. Paulo _____ .
3. Sandra _____ .
4. Sandra _____ .

3. Speaking

Read the survey. Write questions 4 and 5. Complete the survey for yourself. Then ask a classmate the questions.

What can you do?	You		Your classmate	
	Yes	No	Yes	No
1. Can you skateboard?	☐	☐	☐	☐
2. Can you draw?	☐	☐	☐	☐
3. Can you play Ping-Pong?	☐	☐	☐	☐
4. _____	☐	☐	☐	☐
5. _____	☐	☐	☐	☐

Can you skateboard?
Yes, I can. No, I can't.

4. Pronunciation *can* and *can't*

A Listen to the pronunciation of *can* and *can't*.

T.146

He **can** sing.   He **can't** dance.

B Listen and check (✓) *can* or *can't*. Then listen again and practice.

T.147

1. ☐ can   2. ☐ can   3. ☐ can   4. ☐ can   5. ☐ can
   ☐ can't   ☐ can't   ☐ can't   ☐ can't   ☐ can't

Lessons 29 & 30 Mini-review

1. Language check

A Write a question and answer for each picture.

1. Can she sing?
   No, she can't.

2. _____

3. _____

4. _____

B Match the questions to the answers.

1. What's your home like? _b_
2. Can you swim? ____
3. What's your best friend like? ____
4. Is your English class interesting? ____
5. What's your country like? ____
6. Can your teacher play soccer? ____

a. She's fun and really friendly.
b. It's nice. It has four bedrooms.
c. Yes, I can. It's really fun!
d. Yes, it is. And my teacher is nice, too.
e. No, she can't. But she can play tennis.
f. It's beautiful. But some places are busy.

C Now ask and answer the questions in Part B. Give your own information.

What's your home like?   It's . . . .

104   Unit 8

D What's each place like? Write sentences about the places.

- ☐ beautiful
- ☐ busy
- ☑ fun
- ☐ boring
- ☐ exciting
- ☐ interesting

Ipanema Beach

Q: What's it like?
A: *It's fun.*

Paris, France

Q: What's it like?
A: _____

New York City

Q: What's it like?
A: _____

Amusement Park

Q: _____
A: _____

The Museum of Modern Art

Q: _____
A: _____

the bus stop

Q: _____
A: _____

2. Listening

Listen to the conversations. Circle the correct answers.
T.148

1. He (can / can't) sing.
2. She (can / can't) dance.
3. He (can / can't) play Ping-Pong.
4. They (can / can't) draw.
5. She (can / can't) play the guitar.
6. They (can / can't) skateboard.

Time for a Game?
See page 121.

Teen Time

Lesson 31: School fashion

1. Vocabulary

A These three students want new school uniforms. Listen and write their names under the correct pictures.

☐ Mateo ☐ Min ☐ George

blouse, sweater, skirt, shoes

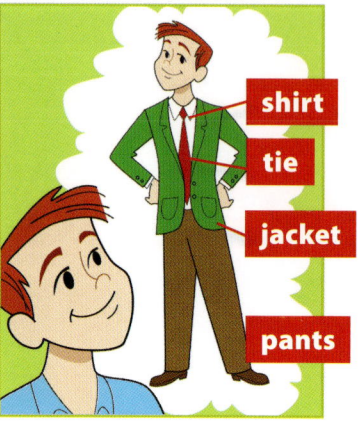

shirt, tie, jacket, pants

T-shirt, shorts, socks, sneakers

B Listen and practice.

C Look at the colors. Listen and practice.

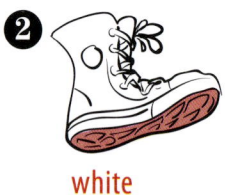

1. blue
2. white
3. green
4. pink
5. orange
6. red
7. black
8. brown
9. yellow
10. purple

D Look at Part A. Complete the descriptions of the school uniforms.

adjective + noun
white blouse
black shoes

1. Min's school uniform is a __pink__ blouse, a blue __skirt__, __black__ shoes, and a blue __sweater__.
2. George's school uniform is a _____ shirt, a green _____, a _____ tie, and _____ pants.
3. Mateo's school uniform is a _____ T-shirt, _____ shorts, yellow _____, and _____ sneakers.

Unit 8

2. Language focus

A Charlie and Lucas talk about their new school uniform. Listen and practice.

What color is / are . . . ?
What color is the shirt? It's white.
What color are the pants? They're blue.

Charlie Oh, wow! There's a new school uniform for next year.
Lucas Really? What's it like?
Charlie It's OK. There's a shirt, a jacket, and pants.
Lucas What color is the shirt?
Charlie It's white.
Lucas That's nice. What color are the pants?
Charlie They're blue.
Lucas And what color is the jacket?
Charlie It's purple.
Lucas Purple? Oh, no!
Charlie Lucas, I'm kidding. The jacket is blue, too.

B What is your dream uniform like? Complete the questions with *is* or *are*. Then answer the questions. Tell your classmates.

1. What color ___is___ the shirt? *It's orange.*
2. What color _____ the pants? _____
3. What color _____ the socks? _____
4. What color _____ the sweater? _____
5. What color _____ the shoes? _____

> The shirt is orange. The pants are . . .

3. Listening

Four students talk on the radio about school fashion. Listen and number the pictures.

Lesson 32 — Teen tastes

1. Vocabulary

A Read about students' favorite things. Match the photos to the correct sentences. Then listen and practice.

- ☐ My favorite music is rap.
- ☐ My favorite school subject is biology.
- [1] My favorite food is pizza.
- ☐ My favorite food is hot dogs.
- ☐ My favorite music is rock.
- ☐ My favorite music is classical.
- ☐ My favorite school subject is Italian.
- ☐ My favorite food is hamburgers.

B Complete these statements. Then tell your classmates.

My favorite music is _____.

My favorite school subject is _____.

My favorite food is _____.

> My favorite music is . . .

108   Unit 8

2. Language focus

A What do Yoshi and Jenny like? Listen and practice.

love / like / don't like
I **love** rock music.
I **like** rap music.
I **don't like** classical music.

I'm a big music fan. I love rock music, and I like rap music. I can play the electric guitar. I don't like classical music. I think it's boring. My friends and I have a rock band. It's really cool.

Yoshi

I love school! I really like all of my classes, and I like my teachers and my friends. The food in the cafeteria is great. There are hot dogs and hamburgers. There's one thing I don't like about school – the homework!

Jenny

B What about you? Complete the statements with *love*, *like*, or *don't like*. Then compare with a classmate.

1. I _____ rap music.
2. I _____ math.
3. I _____ soccer.
4. I _____ pizza.
5. I _____ English.
6. I _____ the beach.
7. I _____ the first day of school.
8. I _____ classical music.
9. I _____ hot dogs.
10. I _____ my first name.
11. I _____ my city / town.
12. I _____ my school.

I love rap music. I think it's cool.

I don't like rap music. I think it's boring.

3. Listening

Nicole talks about her favorite things. Listen and check (✓) the correct things.

Sport	Music	School subject	Food	Clothing
✓ volleyball	☐ rap	☐ art	☐ hamburgers	☐ jacket
☐ tennis	☐ rock	☐ science	☐ pizza	☐ sneakers

Teen Time 109

UNIT 8 Get Connected

Read

A Read the article quickly. Write three things you can do at a New York City street fair.

1. _____ 3. _____
2. _____

New York City Street Fairs

What are New York City street **fairs** like? Well, they're really fun. Some fairs are small **block** or neighborhood parties. But some fairs are really big – 30 city blocks long! There's great food, good music, and a lot of **shopping**.

So, is the shopping good? Yes! The shopping is awesome – and **cheap**. And there are some really nice things. You can **buy** bags, T-shirts, sneakers, CDs, toys – everything!

Are you a big music fan? At some street fairs, you can walk around and listen to music. There's rock, rap, and **jazz**, too!

And, there's a lot of good food, too – pizza, hot dogs, and ice cream. There's food from all around the world. You can eat Italian, Thai, Mexican, Chinese food, and more.

So, go to a street fair for an exciting time! It's crowded, but it's fun!

More Vocabulary Practice? See page 125.

B 🎧 T.157 Read the article slowly. Check your answers in Part A.

C Are these statements true or false? Write *True* or *False*. Then correct the false statements.

1. All New York City street fairs are really big.
   False. *Some New York City street fairs are small.*

2. You can buy a lot of really cool things there.
   _____

3. You can't listen to music at a street fair.
   _____

4. There's only American food at street fairs.
   _____

5. A street fair is exciting, fun, and crowded.
   _____

What's it like?

Listen

A 🎧 T.158 Jessica and Ruben are talking about the school fair. Listen and answer the questions.

1. Is the school fair on Friday? *No, it's on Saturday.*
2. What's the school fair like? _____
3. Can Jessica juggle? _____
4. What colors are the school colors? _____
5. Can Ruben sing? _____

B What do you think? Write *I agree* or *I disagree* (don't agree).

1. School fairs are fun. _____
2. Talent shows are exciting. _____
3. Pizza, hot dogs, and hamburgers are healthy. _____
4. Races are cool. _____

Your turn

Write

A Answer the questions about a fair (or event) at your school, or in your neighborhood or city.

1. What's the name of the fair / event? _____
2. When is it? _____
3. Where is it? _____
4. What can you do there? _____
5. What's it like? _____

B Write about the fair or event. Use the answers in Part A to help you.

I really like the _____

Teen Time 111

UNIT 8 Review

Language chart review

What's . . . like?	love / like / don't like	can / can't
What's New York like? 　It's fun. **What color is / are . . . ?** What color is Kate's sweater? 　It's blue. What color are Kate's shoes? 　They're black.	I love this town. I like the mall. I don't like my room.	I can sing. He can't sing. Can you sing? 　Yes, I can. / No, I can't. Can they play soccer? 　Yes, they can. / No, they can't. can't = cannot

A Amy meets Ivan. Complete the conversation with the sentences in the box. Write the letters in the boxes.

☐ a. I can play the guitar. I'm pretty good.
☐ b. Well, I love soccer, but there are no soccer fields near here.
☑ c. Yes, I am. I'm Ivan.
☐ d. No, I can't. I don't like baseball. Can you play?
☐ e. It's great! The people are friendly, and there are a lot of beautiful places.
☐ f. Yeah, it's interesting. But this town is boring.

Amy　Excuse me. Are you Jon's cousin from Mexico?
Ivan　[c]
Amy　Hi, I'm Amy. So, what's Mexico like?
Ivan　[ ]
Amy　Wow, that's cool! Do you like the U.S.?
Ivan　[ ]
Amy　Really? Why is it boring? I love our town.
Ivan　[ ]
Amy　Yeah, you're right. But there's a baseball field. Can you play baseball?
Ivan　[ ]
Amy　Yes, I can. I love baseball. So, what other things can you do?
Ivan　[ ]
Amy　Really? I can play the guitar, too.

B What do you think Ivan and Amy say? Circle the correct words.

Ivan
1. I (like / don't like) the U.S.
2. I (like / don't like) this town.
3. I (can / can't) play baseball.

Amy
4. I (can / can't) play baseball.
5. I (like / don't like) this town.
6. I (like / don't like) music.

C Look at the picture on page 112. What are Amy's clothes like? What are Ivan's clothes like? Circle the false sentences.

1. (Ivan's pants are brown.)
2. Amy's T-shirt is red.
3. Ivan's shirt is white.
4. Amy's skirt is blue.
5. Amy's shoes are green.
6. Ivan's sneakers are purple.
7. Amy's hat is blue.
8. Ivan's jacket is black.

D Now correct the false sentences in Part C.

1. Ivan's pants are black.
2. _____
3. _____
4. _____

E Write the questions or the answers about Andrea.

1. **Q:** What color is Andrea's blouse?
   A: It's white.
2. **Q:** What color are Andrea's pants?
   A: _____
3. **Q:** _____
   A: It's green.
4. **Q:** What color is Andrea's sweater?
   A: _____
5. **Q:** _____
   A: They're pink.
6. **Q:** What color is Andrea's hat?
   A: _____

F Write questions beginning with *Can you*. Then answer the questions with your own information.

1. (sing) **Q:** Can you sing?
   A: _____
2. (skateboard) **Q:** _____
   A: _____
3. (draw people) **Q:** _____
   A: _____
4. (play tennis) **Q:** _____
   A: _____

Time for the Theme Project? See page 133.

Teen Time 113

UNIT 1 Game *Connect It!*

A Connect the words in the maze to make five sentences.

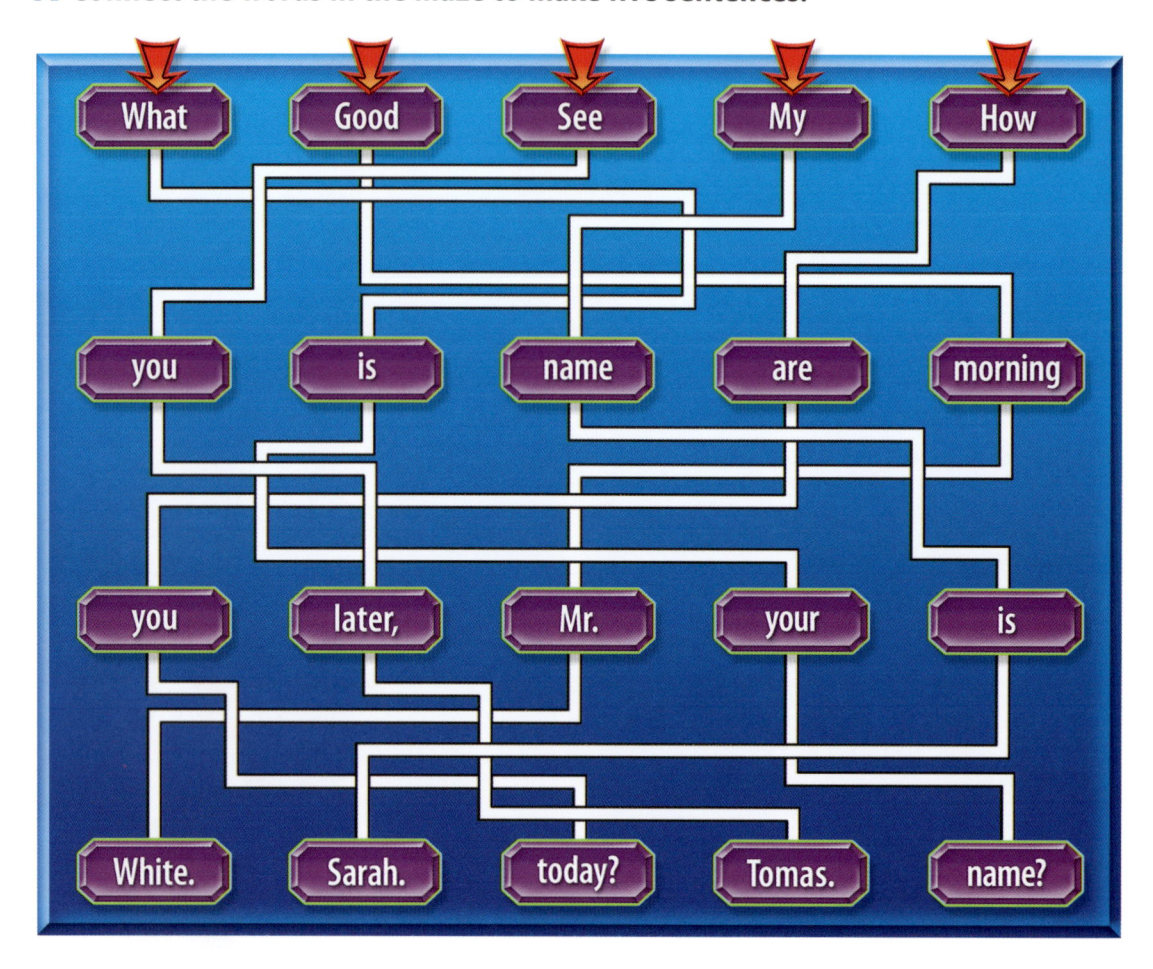

[Maze with words: What, Good, See, My, How / you, is, name, are, morning / you, later,, Mr., your, is / White., Sarah., today?, Tomas., name?]

B Complete the conversations with four sentences from Part A.

1. **A** _____
   B Hello, Todd.
2. **A** _____
   B Fine, thanks.
3. **A** _____
   B Bye-bye.
4. **A** _____
   B My name is Sarah.

C Now practice with a classmate. Use your own information.

What's your name?   My name is . . . .

114   Unit 1 Game

UNIT 2 Game *Crossword puzzle*

Look at the pictures to complete the crossword.

6 across: BESTFRIEND

Across

2. Mr. Armstrong is a great _____ .
6. Josh is my _____ .
7. Mike isn't a tennis player. He's a _____ .
8. Tasha Reed is my favorite _____ .

Down

1. Mr. Brooks isn't a science teacher. He's a _____ .
3. Margie Frick is in good movies. She's my favorite _____ .
4. My favorite song is *In the World*. The _____ is Daniela Ella.
5. Jackie is my _____ . She's my science lab partner, too.

Unit 2 Game 115

UNIT 3   Game *What's this?*

A What are these objects? Guess. Label each photo.

1. a computer
2.
3.
4.
5.
6.
7.
8.
9.
10.
11.
12.

B How many of your answers are correct? Compare with a classmate.

You What's this?
Classmate I think it's a computer.
You I think it's a television.

UNIT 4 Game *Find the differences*

How is Picture 2 different from Picture 1? Complete the chart.

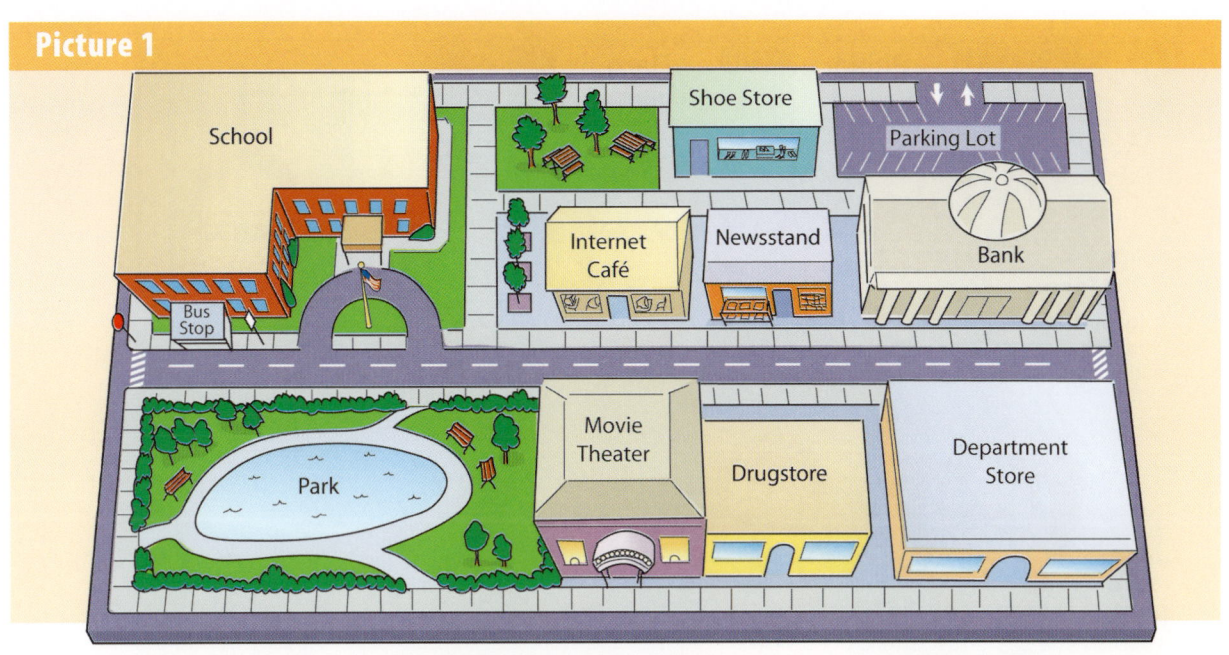

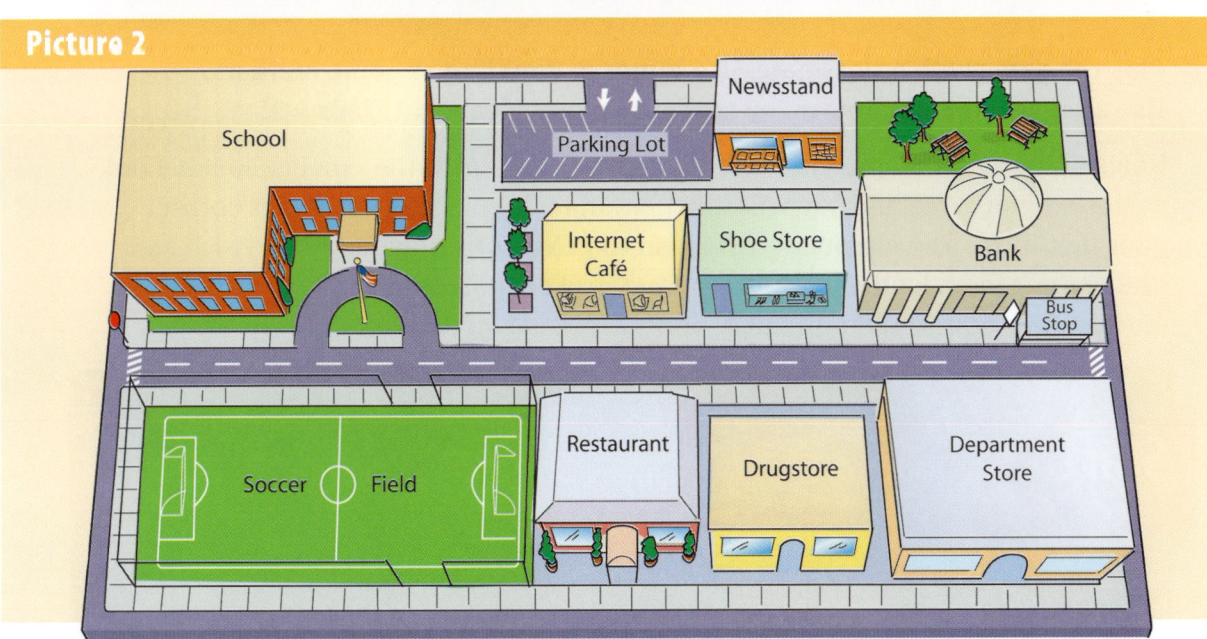

Picture 1

Picture 2

Picture 1	Picture 2
The bus stop is in front of the school.	The bus stop is in front of the bank.
The school is across from the park.	
The parking lot is behind the bank.	
The newsstand is in front of the shoe store.	
The drugstore is between the movie theater and the department store.	

UNIT 5 Game *Who's this?*

A Look at Ron's family tree. Who are the people in his family?

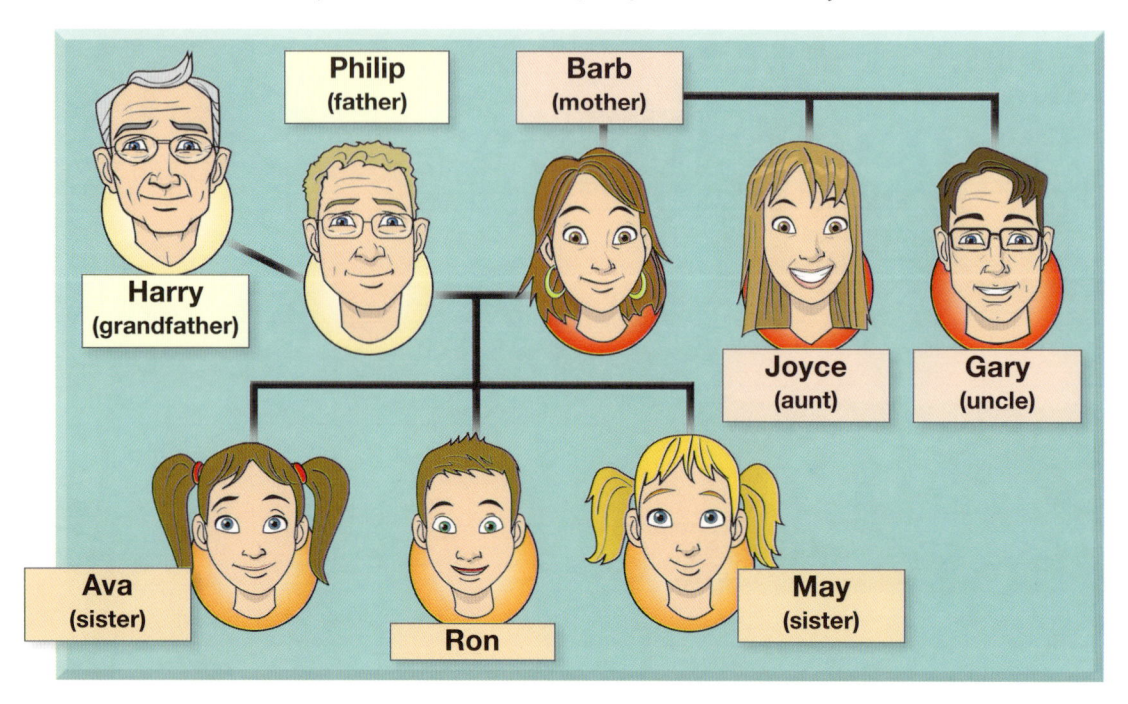

Philip (father)
Barb (mother)
Harry (grandfather)
Joyce (aunt)
Gary (uncle)
Ava (sister)
Ron
May (sister)

B Play the game with a classmate. Use things in your bag as game markers. Use a coin to find out how many spaces to move. Heads = 1, Tails = 2.

Rules: Take turns. Flip a coin and move your marker to the correct space. Look at Ron's family tree and say who the person is. If your answer is not correct, you lose your next turn. The classmate who gets to FINISH first, wins.

Classmate 1 (coin landed on heads): *Barb is Ron's mother.*
Classmate 2 (coin landed on tails): *Harry is Ron's grandfather.*

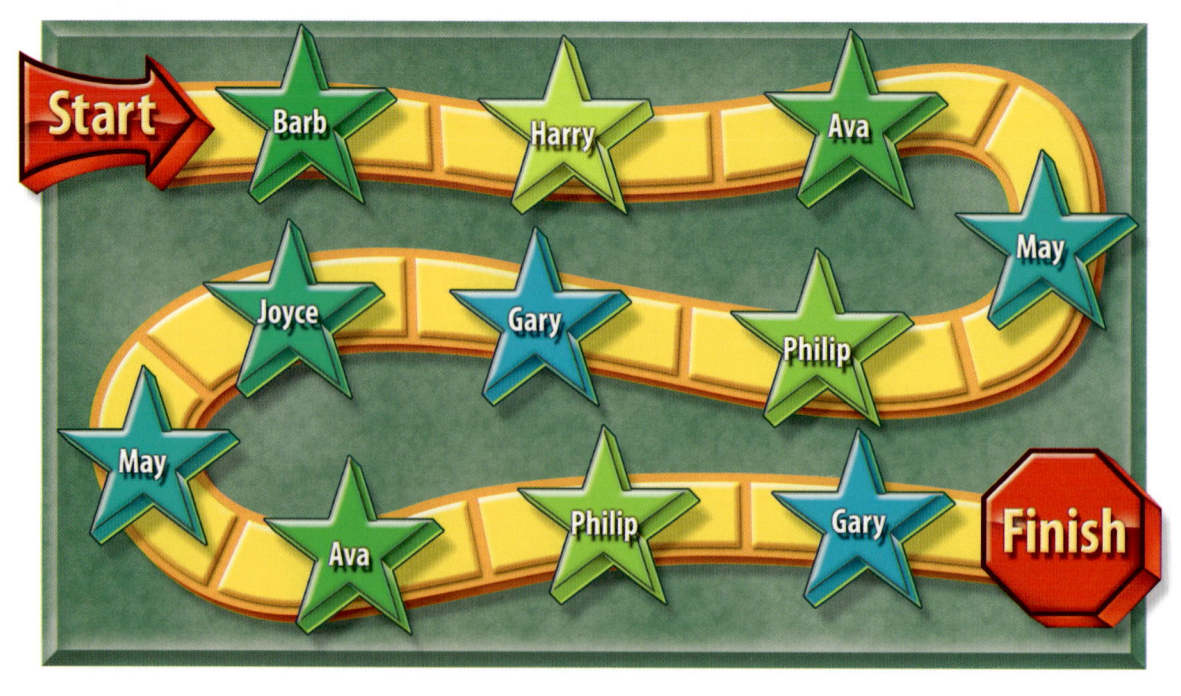

Start — Barb — Harry — Ava — May — Philip — Gary — Joyce — May — Ava — Philip — Gary — Finish

118   Unit 5 Game

UNIT 6 Game *Do you remember?*

**Look at the picture for one minute. Close your book.
Your teacher asks questions. What do you remember?**

Teacher Are there any tables?	**Teacher** Is there a tennis court?
Team A Yes, there are.	**Team B** No, there isn't.

UNIT 7 Game *Countries puzzle*

A Write the missing letters to make country names.

A <u>u s t r a l i</u> a
B ___ ___ ___ l
C ___ ___ ___ ___ a
E ___ ___ ___ ___ ___ ___ d
F ___ ___ ___ ___ ___ e
I ___ ___ ___ a
M ___ ___ ___ ___ o
S ___ ___ ___ n

B Write the country names from Part A to complete the puzzle.

8 A U S T R A L I A

UNIT 8 Game *Can you...?*

Play the game with a classmate. Use things in your bag as game markers.
Use a coin to find out how many spaces to move. Heads = 1, Tails = 2.

Rules:
- Take turns. Flip a coin and move to the correct space.
- Read the question. Can you do what it says?
    - ▶ Yes. Follow the green arrow and move ahead.
    - ◀ No. Follow the purple arrow and move back.
- On a "free space," ask a classmate any question. Keep your marker on that space until your next turn.
- The person who gets to FINISH first, wins.

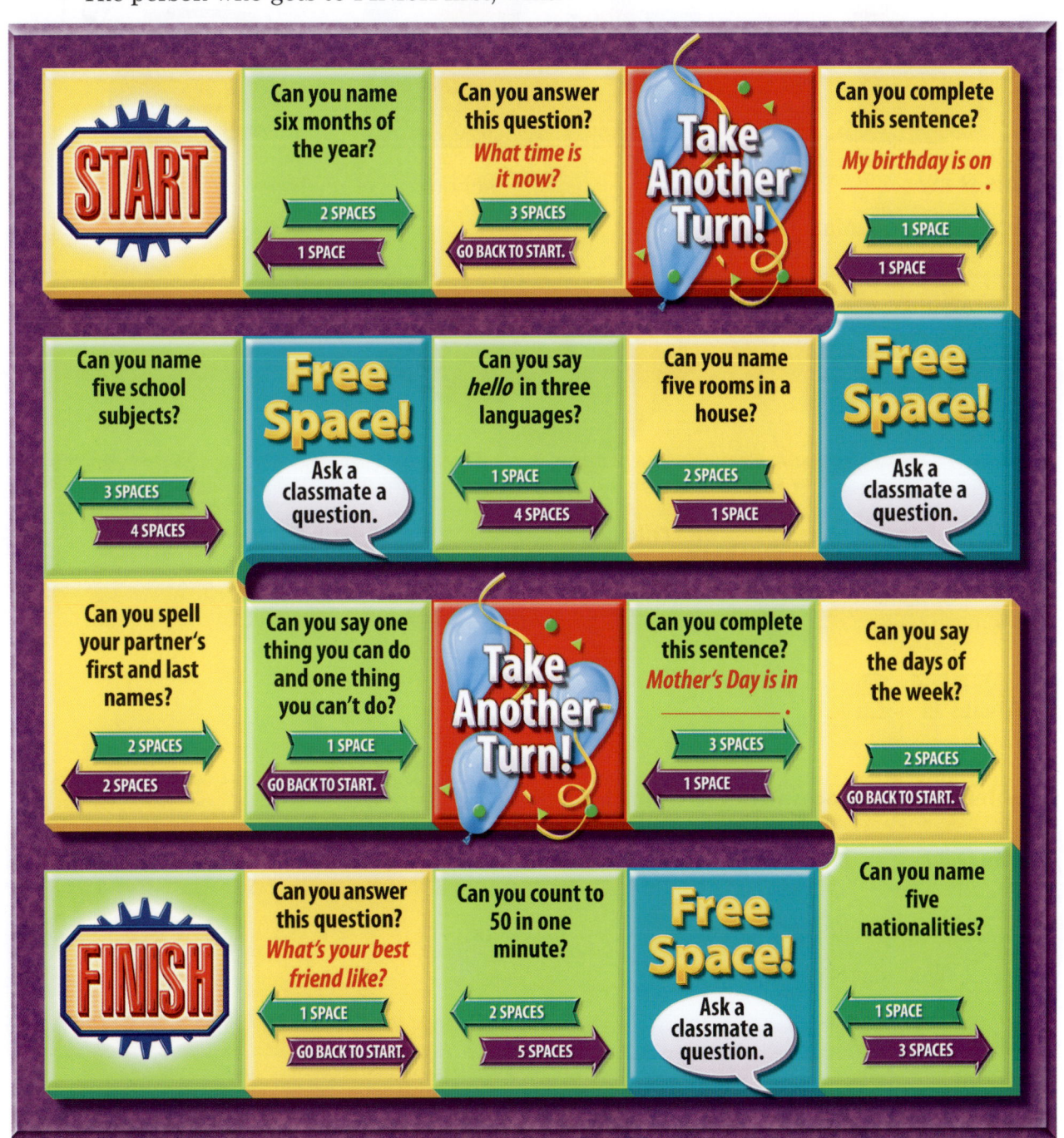

START

Can you name six months of the year?
→ 2 SPACES
← 1 SPACE

Can you answer this question? *What time is it now?*
→ 3 SPACES
← GO BACK TO START.

Take Another Turn!

Can you complete this sentence? *My birthday is on _____.*
→ 1 SPACE
← 1 SPACE

Can you name five school subjects?
→ 3 SPACES
← 4 SPACES

Free Space! Ask a classmate a question.

Can you say *hello* in three languages?
→ 1 SPACE
← 4 SPACES

Can you name five rooms in a house?
→ 2 SPACES
← 1 SPACE

Free Space! Ask a classmate a question.

Can you spell your partner's first and last names?
→ 2 SPACES
← 2 SPACES

Can you say one thing you can do and one thing you can't do?
→ 1 SPACE
← GO BACK TO START.

Take Another Turn!

Can you complete this sentence? *Mother's Day is in _____.*
→ 3 SPACES
← 1 SPACE

Can you say the days of the week?
→ 2 SPACES
← GO BACK TO START.

FINISH

Can you answer this question? *What's your best friend like?*
→ 1 SPACE
← GO BACK TO START.

Can you count to 50 in one minute?
→ 2 SPACES
← 5 SPACES

Free Space! Ask a classmate a question.

Can you name five nationalities?
→ 1 SPACE
← 3 SPACES

Get Connected Vocabulary Practice

UNIT 1

Complete the sentences with the words in the box.

☐ candy bar (n.)   ☑ dog (n.)   ☐ like (v.)   ☐ music (n.)   ☐ sushi (n.)

1. This is my ___dog___ , Max.

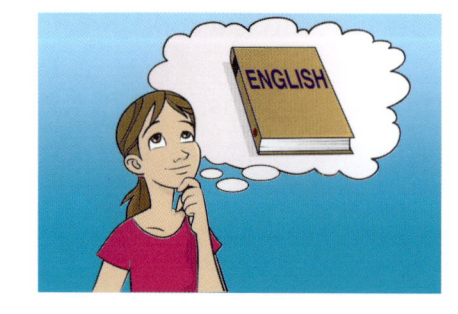

2. I _____ school.

3. That _____ is great.

4. I like _____ .

5. This is a great _____ .

UNIT 2

Complete the sentences with the words in the box.

☐ cute (adj.)   ☐ beautiful (adj.)   ☐ show (n.)   ☑ sport (n.)

1. My favorite ___sport___ is tennis.
2. That cartoon is so _____ .
3. My favorite _____ is on TV now.
4. This _____ model is from Brazil.

UNIT 3

Complete the sentences with the words in the box.

| ☐ cat (n.) | ☐ spider (n.) | ☐ tree house (n.) |
| ☐ smiles (v.) | ☑ teenager (n.) | ☐ virtual (adj.) |

1. Marc is 13. He's a _____teenager_____ .
2. It's not a dog – it's a _____ .
3. He has posters, a chair, and books in his _____ .
4. My friend's pet is weird. It's a _____ .
5. Look at this _____ room on my Web site. It's cool.
6. She _____ a lot. She's very happy.

UNIT 4

Match the sentences to the correct pictures.

1. That bookstore is the <u>biggest (adj.)</u> one. __c__

2. <u>Paintball (n.)</u> is really cool. ____

3. <u>Waterslides (n.)</u> are fun. ____

4. A <u>jungle (n.)</u> is interesting. ____

5. Let's go to the <u>amusement park (n.)</u>. ____

a.

b.

c.

d.

e.

UNIT 5

Complete the sentences with the words in the box.

☐ different (adj.)   ☐ lucky (adj.)   ☐ run (v.)
☐ homeschooled (adj.)   ☐ oldest (adj.)   ☑ youngest (adj.)

1. My little sister is the ____youngest____ child in my family.
2. I don't live with my grandparents. They live in a _____ city.
3. Let's _____ in the park together.
4. My friends and family are great! I'm so _____ .
5. His mother is his teacher and his school is at
   home. He's _____ .
6. My _____ cousin is 25. My youngest cousin is 5.

UNIT 6

The underlined words belong in other sentences. Write the words where they belong.

1. <u>Summer (n.)</u> with tennis balls is really fun. ____Juggling____
2. That famous model studies <u>summer camp (n.)</u>. _____
3. There are <u>juggling (n.)</u> classes in the computer lab. _____
4. The <u>3D animation (n.)</u> classes are in the school kitchen. _____
5. <u>Fashion design (n.)</u> is really cool. There are volleyball games,
   contests, art classes, talent shows, picnics, and more! _____
6. In <u>cooking (n.)</u>, people go to the beach a lot. _____

124   Get Connected Vocabulary Practice

UNIT 7

Complete the sentences with the words in the box.

> ☐ celebrations (n.) ☑ receive (v.) ☐ windows (n.)
> ☐ important (adj.) ☐ throw (v.)

1. People __receive__ a lot of cards and candy on Valentine's Day.
2. Thanksgiving is a very _____ holiday in America.
3. There are two big _____ in my bedroom.
4. On July 4th, there are many _____ in the U.S.
5. Kids think it is fun to _____ water at each other at the beach.

UNIT 8

Complete the advertisement with the words in the box.

> ☐ blocks (n.) ☐ cheap (adj.) ☐ jazz (n.)
> ☐ buy (v.) ☑ Fair (n.) ☐ shopping (v.)

Come to the City Park __Fair__ this Saturday, May 5th! It's five city _____ long! The _____ is great – there are T-shirts, CDs, posters, and other things. You can listen to rock and _____, too. _____ your favorite foods – they're _____, but good. See you Saturday from 11:00 a.m. to 4:00 p.m. for a fun day at the fair!

Get Connected Vocabulary Practice

UNIT 1

Theme Project: Make a personal information poster.
Theme: Relationships
Goal: To create stronger relationships in your classroom community

At Home

Read about Andréia.

My first name is Andréia. My last name is Lima. My nickname is Déia. My e-mail address is andreialima789@school.dt.br. My favorite subject is science.

Complete the sentence. Use your dictionary, if necessary.

My favorite school subject is _____.

Draw a picture or bring a photo of yourself to class.

In Class

Make a poster. Ask each other *What's your . . . ?* Write the answers. Use the sample poster as a model.

Choose a group leader. Present your poster to another group.

This is Megumi.

Hi, Megumi.

Hello. This is my picture. My last name is Ohno. My nickname is Meg. My e-mail address is megumio@school.net. My favorite subject is math.

Display the posters in your classroom. Walk around and look at all of them. Who has an interesting nickname?

Photo				
First name	Megumi	Andrew	Maria	Luciano de
Last name	Ohno	Smith	Valdez	Almeida
Nickname	Meg	Andy	Mari	Lú
E-mail address	megumio135@school.dt.br	andysmith98@school.dt.br	mari586@school.dt.br	lucianolu268@school.dt.br
Favorite subject	math	English	social studies	science

Sample poster

UNIT 2

Theme Project: Make a poster about two people who work at your school.
Theme: Citizenship
Goal: To become better acquainted with people in your school community

At Home

Read about Mr. Alvarez.

This is Mr. Alvarez. His first name is Pedro. He's a math teacher at my school. He's from Juarez. His favorite tennis player is Rafael Nadal.

Mr. Alvarez

Before Class

Talk to a worker at your school. Complete the chart. Use your dictionary, if necessary.

First name	Last name	Hometown	Job	Favorite

Draw a picture or bring a photo of the worker to class.

In Class

- Look at all the people. Choose the two most interesting people.
- Make a poster. Use the sample poster as a model.
- Choose a group leader. Present your poster to another group.

This is Mr. Ramirez. His first name is Pablo. He's a soccer coach. He's from Guadalajara. His favorite soccer player is Nery Castillo.

This is Ms. Lopez. Her first name is . . .

Name: Pablo Ramirez (Mr. Ramirez)
Job: soccer coach
Hometown: Guadalajara

Name: Carmen Lopez (Ms. Lopez)
Job: science teacher
Hometown: Monterrey

Sample poster

- Display the posters in your classroom. Walk around and look at all of them. How many people do you know?

Unit 2 Theme Project 127

UNIT 3

Theme Project: Make an advertisement for an electronics store.
Theme: Consumer awareness
Goal: To become aware of the powerful influence of advertising

At Home

Read about Paulo's favorite electronic things.

> Look at my favorite electronic things. This is my laptop. It's new. This is my MP3 player. It's a radio, too. And this is my cell phone. Look! It's a camera, too. It's really cool.

Think of three electronic things. Write the names of the things. Use your dictionary, if necessary.

1. _____ 2. _____ 3. _____

Find advertisements for the three electronic things you wrote. Look in newspapers and magazines. Bring the advertisements to class.

In Class

- Look at all the advertisements. Choose five things. Choose the coolest advertisements for them.

- Choose a name for your electronics store. Make an advertisement. Use the sample advertisement as a model.

- Choose a group leader. Present your advertisement to another group.

> This is Steph's Electronics Store. Look at the cool things in the store! This is an MP3 player. That's a . . .

- Display the advertisements in your classroom. Walk around and look at all of them. Vote on the coolest one.

Steph's Electronics Store
Cool things for everybody!

Sample store advertisement

128   Unit 3 Theme Project

UNIT 4

Theme Project: Make a guide for visitors to your city.
Theme: Citizenship
Goal: To learn more about your city or town; to provide useful information for visitors

At Home

Read about John's hometown and his suggestions for visitors.

Welcome to my city – Chicago! Go to the John Hancock Tower. It's on Michigan Avenue. It's really tall. Go to the top – it's a great view. Water Tower Place is also on Michigan Avenue. It's a big mall. Have a sandwich there and do some shopping. My favorite bookstore is across from Water Tower Place. Read a magazine there and have a soda there. Let's go together sometime!

John Hancock Tower   Water Tower Place

What places in your city or town should a visitor know about? Complete the chart. Use your dictionary, if necessary.

Place: _____   Place: _____

Location: _____   Location: _____

Suggestion: _____   Suggestion: _____

Draw pictures or bring photos of the places to class.

In Class

- Look at all the places. Choose two places.
- Make a page for a guide on a piece of paper. Use the sample page as a model.
- Choose a group leader. Present your places to another group.

> Go to Pike Place Market. It's on Pike Street. Have a sandwich and a soda there.

- Give your group's page to the teacher. The teacher staples together the pages. Pass around the guide. What is your favorite place? Why?

Pike Place Market
Pike Street
Have a sandwich and a soda!

Space Needle
Seattle Center
Go to the top!

Sample guide page

Unit 4 Theme Project 129

UNIT 5

Theme Project: Make a group photo album.
Themes: Relationships; multiculturalism
Goal: To create stronger relationships in your classroom community

At Home

Read about Tomoko's favorite relative.

My name is Tomoko Fuji. I have a lot of nice relatives. My favorite relative is my uncle. His name is Hiro. He's my mother's brother. He's 46. He's smart and really funny. I think he's handsome, too!

Hiro

Complete the chart about your favorite relative. Use your dictionary, if necessary.

Name	Age	Relationship	What's he / she like?

Draw a picture or bring a photo of your favorite relative to class.

In Class

- Make a photo album page of your relative. Use the sample album page as a model.
- Tell your group about your relative.

  This is my cousin, Sofia. She's 21. She's tall and thin. She's really friendly. Sofia is my favorite relative.

- Make a group photo album. Make a cover for your photo album. Then staple together all of your pages and the cover to make your album.
- Choose a group leader. Present your photo album to another group.
- Display the photo albums in your classroom. Walk around and look at all of them. Which person do you want to meet? Why?

Sofia
Cousin, 21

Sample photo album page

UNIT 6

Theme Project: Make a poster of a dream school ("cool school").
Theme: Citizenship
Goal: To learn to present an idea for an ideal school

At Home

Read about Kevin's ideas for his "cool school."

> My cool school is great! There's an auditorium in the school. We have juggling class there. There's a football field in the school. We have marching band there. There's a computer lab in the school. We have Web design class there. I love my school!

Think of your "cool school." What facilities does it have? What classes does it have? Complete the chart. Use your dictionary, if necessary.

Facility	Class
1.	
2.	
3.	

Draw pictures or bring photos of the facilities to class.

In Class

- Choose three subjects for classes at your "cool school." Choose a facility to have each subject.
- Make a poster. Use the sample poster as a model.
- Choose a group leader. Present your poster to another group.

> This is our "cool school." There is a media center in our school. We have film-making class there . . .

- Display the posters in your classroom. Walk around and look at all of them. Vote on the best "cool school."

Media center
Film-making

Soccer field
Soccer

Swimming pool
Swimming

Sample poster

Unit 6 Theme Project 131

UNIT 7

Theme Project: Make an informational booklet about different countries.
Theme: Cultural diversity
Goal: To learn about different countries and cultures

At Home

Read about Kenya.

- Kenya is in Africa. There are mountains in Kenya. Mt. Kenya is a very famous mountain. There are lions, elephants, and other wild animals in Kenya.
- Kenyan people speak English and Swahili.
- Jamhuri is Kenyan Independence Day. It is on December 12th. There are parades and fireworks.
- Mercy Myra is a famous Kenyan. She's a singer.

Mount Kenya

Choose a country. Complete the chart. Use your dictionary, if necessary.

Country: _____   Important day: _____

Continent: _____   Famous person: _____

Language: _____   Other: _____

Draw pictures or bring photos of the country you chose to class.

In Class

1. Make a page for the country you chose. Use the sample page as a model.

2. Tell your group about your country.

   > South Korea is in Asia. Korean people speak Korean . . .

3. Make a group booklet. Make a cover for your booklet. Then staple together all of your pages and the cover to make your booklet.

4. Choose a group leader. Present your booklet to another group.

5. Display the booklets in your classroom. Walk around and look at all of them. Vote on the most interesting booklet.

> South Korea is in Asia. Korean people speak Korean. Students study Korean – and English, too. Korean New Year is a big holiday. It starts on a different day every year. It is usually in February. BoA is a famous Korean. She is a singer.

Sample informational booklet page

UNIT 8

Theme Project: Make a pair of bookmarks of healthy foods and activities.
Theme: Health and fitness
Goal: To become more aware of healthy foods and activities

At Home

Read about the health tips.

It's great to be healthy. So, eat healthy foods and do healthy activities. Potato chips and candy aren't healthy snacks. Choose healthy ones – eat an apple or a carrot.

Choose healthy activities, too. Ride your bike to school or play basketball on the weekend. Be active – it's good for you!

Write three healthy foods and three healthy activities. Use your dictionary, if necessary.

Healthy foods	Healthy activities
1.	1.
2.	2.
3.	3.

In Class

- Look at all the lists.
- Choose one food and one activity you like. Make two bookmarks. Use the sample bookmarks as models.
- Present your bookmarks to your group.

  > Eat bananas. They're healthy. Walk to school. It's good for you!

- Display all the bookmarks in your classroom. Walk around and look at all of them. What are your favorite healthy foods and activities?

Eat bananas. They're healthy.

Walk to school. It's good for you!

Sample bookmarks

Unit 8 Theme Project

Word List

Esta lista inclui as palavras e as frases-chave do *Connect Revised Edition* Combo 1. O número que aparece ao lado de cada palavra se refere à página do Student's Book em que elas aparecem pela primeira vez.

Key Vocabulary

Aa
a (19) _____
about (5) _____
across from (46) _____
actor (18) _____
address book (30) _____
after (8) _____
after [for time] (80) _____
afternoon (4) _____
age (22) _____
alarm clock (32) _____
all (87) _____
alphabet [a–z] (10) _____
already (81) _____
also (33) _____
always (95) _____
am (2) _____
American (88) _____
amusement park (54) _____
an (32) _____
and (17) _____
animals (100) _____
any (52) _____
apartment (64) _____
April (92) _____
are (5) _____
around (28) _____
art (78) _____
at (28) _____
at all (103) _____
athletic field (74) _____
auditorium (74) _____
August (92) _____
aunt (58) _____
Australia (25) _____
Australia Day (93) _____
Australian (88) _____
avenue (46) _____

Bb
back (2) _____
backpack (30) _____
bad (5) _____
bag (30) _____
band concert (80) _____
bank (46) _____
baseball (74) _____
basketball (16) _____

bathroom (66) _____
beach (52) _____
beautiful (26) _____
bed (38) _____
bedroom (66) _____
behind (46) _____
Belize (86) _____
best friend (16) _____
between (46) _____
bicycle (36) _____
big (64) _____
biggest (54) _____
biology (108) _____
birthday (22) _____
black (106) _____
block (110) _____
blouse (106) _____
blue (106) _____
board (72) _____
book (30) _____
bookcase (72) _____
bookstore (50) _____
bored (52) _____
boring (84) _____
bowling alley (50) _____
boy (87) _____
Brazil (24) _____
Brazilian (88) _____
British (88) _____
brother (37) _____
brown (106) _____
brush (30) _____
burger (76) _____
bus stop (44) _____
busy (100) _____
but (31) _____
buy (110) _____
bye (9) _____
bye-bye (9) _____

Cc
cabinet (72) _____
café (28) _____
cafeteria (74) _____
calculator (32) _____
camera (30) _____
can (28) _____
Canada (25) _____

Canadian (88) _____
candy bar (12) _____
candy store (50) _____
can't (102) _____
card (11) _____
Carnaval (93) _____
cartoon character (18) _____
cat (40) _____
CD / DVD player (72) _____
celebration (96) _____
cell phone (32) _____
chair (38) _____
cheap (110) _____
child (59) _____
children (59) _____
Children's Day (93) _____
Chinese (76) _____
city (64) _____
class (20) _____
classical (music) (108) _____
classmate (2) _____
classroom (64) _____
coach (16) _____
Colombia (24) _____
Colombian (89) _____
color (107) _____
come (84) _____
comic book (36) _____
computer lab (74) _____
computer partner (16) _____
cooking (82) _____
cool (32) _____
country (67) _____
cousin (58) _____
crazy (60) _____
cute (19) _____

Dd
Dad (17) _____
dance [verb] (102) _____
day (79) _____
dear (73) _____
December (92) _____
department store (46) _____
desk (38) _____
desktop computer (32) _____
different (68) _____
difficult (78) _____

dining room (66) _____
do (11) _____
dog (12) _____
don't like (108) _____
downtown (46) _____
draw (102) _____
dream (home) (67) _____
dresser (38) _____
drugstore (46) _____

Ee
easy (78) _____
eight (22) _____
eighteen (22) _____
eighteenth (94) _____
eighth (94) _____
eighty (58) _____
electric (guitar) (109) _____
eleven (22) _____
eleventh (94) _____
e-mail (84) _____
England (86) _____
English (65) _____
enter (102) _____
e-pal (24) _____
eraser (30) _____
evening (4) _____
every (79) _____
everybody (51) _____
everyday (30) _____
excited (81) _____
exciting (100) _____

Ff
facility (74) _____
fair (110) _____
family (58) _____
famous (84) _____
fan (19) _____
fashion design (82) _____
fashion show (80) _____
father (58) _____
Father's Day (92) _____
favorite (16) _____
February (92) _____
fifteen (22) _____
fifteenth (94) _____
fifth (94) _____
fifty (58) _____
fine (5) _____
fine arts (84) _____
first (11) _____
five (22) _____
floor (101) _____
food (76) _____
football (74) _____
for (5) _____
forty (58) _____
four (22) _____
fourteen (22) _____
fourteenth (94) _____
fourth (94) _____

France (88) _____
French (88) _____
Friday (79) _____
friend (16) _____
friendly (60) _____
from (24) _____
fun (76) _____
funny (26) _____

Gg
game (80) _____
garage (66) _____
geography (28) _____
girl (87) _____
global (28) _____
go (8) _____
goal (48) _____
good (4) _____
good-bye (9) _____
grandfather (58) _____
grandmother (58) _____
grandparents (58) _____
great (5) _____
green (106) _____
guitar (102) _____
gym (74) _____

Hh
half (past) (80) _____
hamburger (76) _____
handsome (60) _____
happy (64) _____
happy birthday (23) _____
has (59) _____
hat (30) _____
have (59) _____
have (a soda) (52) _____
he (19) _____
health (78) _____
hello (2) _____
her (17) _____
here (11) _____
hey (33) _____
hi (2) _____
him (37) _____
his (17) _____
history (78) _____
holiday (92) _____
home (45) _____
homeschooled (68) _____
homework (109) _____
hot (52) _____
hot dog (108) _____
house (67) _____
how (5) _____
hungry (47) _____
hurry (45) _____

Ii
I (2) _____
idea (53) _____
important (96) _____

in (38) _____
Independence Day (92) _____
India (86) _____
in front of (46) _____
inside (64) _____
interesting (84) _____
international (49) _____
Internet (33) _____
Internet café (44) _____
introduce (87) _____
is (2) _____
it (28) _____
Italian (108) _____

Jj
jacket (106) _____
January (92) _____
Japan (25) _____
Japanese (88) _____
jazz (110) _____
juggling (82) _____
July (92) _____
June (92) _____
jungle (54) _____
just (25) _____

Kk
kangaroo (100) _____
keypad (33) _____
kidding (25) _____
kitchen (66) _____
know (25) _____

Ll
language lab (74) _____
laptop (32) _____
last (11) _____
late (4) _____
later (9) _____
let's (8) _____
letter (65) _____
library (11) _____
like (me) (58) _____
like [verb] (12) _____
like [What's he like?] (61) _____
little (23) _____
little [a little] (61) _____
live [verb] (65) _____
living room (66) _____
look (17) _____
lost (47) _____
lot [a lot] (64) _____
love [verb] (84) _____
lucky (68) _____
lunch (79) _____

Mm
mall (50) _____
many (84) _____
map (47) _____
March (92) _____

math (16) _____
May (92) _____
me (53) _____
media center (72) _____
meet (3) _____
mess [noun] (30) _____
Mexican (88) _____
Mexico (24) _____
middle school (73) _____
minute (28) _____
Miss (4) _____
miss [verb] (64) _____
model (18) _____
Mom (31) _____
Monday (79) _____
money (53) _____
month (95) _____
more (72) _____
morning (4) _____
mother (58) _____
Mother's Day (92) _____
mountain (84) _____
movie (21) _____
movie theater (44) _____
MP3 player (32) _____
Mr. (4) _____
Mrs. (4) _____
Ms. (4) _____
museum (84) _____
music (12) _____
music store (50) _____
my (2) _____

Nn
name (2) _____
national (84) _____
nationality (88) _____
near (45) _____
neighbor (65) _____
neighborhood (64) _____
new (5) _____
newsstand (44) _____
New Year's Eve (92) _____
New Zealand (86) _____
next to (38) _____
next (year) (107) _____
nice (3) _____
night (9) _____
nine (22) _____
nineteen (22) _____
nineteenth (94) _____
ninety (58) _____
ninth (94) _____
no (22) _____
noisy (64) _____
noon (80) _____
not (5) _____
notebook (30) _____
November (92) _____
now (37) _____
number (65) _____

Oo
observatory (101) _____
o'clock (79) _____
October (92) _____
of (25) _____
OK (5) _____
old [adjective] (64) _____
old [age] (23) _____
oldest (68) _____
on (33) _____
one (22) _____
one hundred (58) _____
online (93) _____
only (23) _____
only (child) (59) _____
orange [color] (106) _____
other (75) _____
our (65) _____

Pp
paintball (54) _____
pants (106) _____
parents (58) _____
park (46) _____
parking lot (46) _____
partner (16) _____
party (95) _____
P.E. (78) _____
pen (30) _____
pencil (38) _____
pencil case (30) _____
people (16) _____
Peru (25) _____
Peruvian (88) _____
photo (25) _____
physical education (78) _____
picnic (80) _____
picture (70) _____
Ping-Pong (102) _____
pink (106) _____
pizza (108) _____
place (76) _____
play (52) _____
please (45) _____
popular (88) _____
Portugal (25) _____
poster (36) _____
pretty (60) _____
printer (72) _____
problem (73) _____
Puerto Rican (88) _____
Puerto Rico (88) _____
purple (106) _____

Qq
quarter (after / to) (80) _____
quiet (64) _____
quiz (88) _____

Rr
race (80) _____
radio (107) _____
rap (music) (108) _____
ready (5) _____
really [adverb] (23) _____
really [exclamation] (20) _____
receive (96) _____
red (106) _____
remote control (72) _____
restaurant (44) _____
reunion (60) _____
right (19) _____
right [correct] (11) _____
right now (93) _____
rock band (109) _____
rock (music) (108) _____
run (68) _____

Ss
sad (64) _____
same (37) _____
sandwich (52) _____
Saturday (94) _____
scanner (72) _____
schedule (79) _____
school (2) _____
science (16) _____
screen (72) _____
second (94) _____
see (9) _____
September (92) _____
serious (89) _____
seven (22) _____
seventeen (22) _____
seventeenth (94) _____
seventh (94) _____
seventy (58) _____
she (19) _____
shirt (106) _____
shoes (106) _____
shoe store (44) _____
shopping (110) _____
short (60) _____
shorts (106) _____
shy (60) _____
sing (102) _____
Singapore (86) _____
singer (18) _____
sister (23) _____
sit (down) (52) _____
six (22) _____
sixteen (22) _____
sixteenth (94) _____
sixth (94) _____
sixty (58) _____
skateboard (102) _____
skating rink (50) _____
skirt (106) _____
small (37) _____

smart (60) _____
smile (40) _____
sneakers (106) _____
so [conjunction] (19) _____
so [very] (23) _____
soccer field (48) _____
soccer player (19) _____
socks (106) _____
soda (52) _____
some (89) _____
sometimes (64) _____
soon (4) _____
sorry (49) _____
South Africa (86) _____
South Korea (88) _____
South Korean (88) _____
Spain (88) _____
Spanish [language] (78) _____
Spanish [nationality] (88) _____
speak (87) _____
spell (11) _____
spelling contest (80) _____
spider (40) _____
sports (26) _____
sports facilities (74) _____
Spring Day (80) _____
star [famous person] (18) _____
still (45) _____
street (46) _____
subject (78) _____
subway station (46) _____
suggestion (52) _____
summer (82) _____
summer camp (82) _____
Sunday (94) _____
sushi (12) _____
sweater (106) _____
swimming (52) _____
swimming pool (74) _____

Tt
talent show (102) _____
tall (60) _____
taste (108) _____
teacher (16) _____
team (48) _____
teen (100) _____
teenager (40) _____
television (32) _____
tell (37) _____
ten (22) _____
tennis court (74) _____
tennis player (18) _____
tenth (94) _____
thanks (5) _____
Thanksgiving (92) _____
thank you (5) _____
that (11) _____
the (5) _____
their (65) _____
them (57) _____

there (51) _____
these (37) _____
they (37) _____
thin (60) _____
things (30) _____
think (19) _____
third (94) _____
thirsty (52) _____
thirteen (22) _____
thirteenth (94) _____
thirtieth (94) _____
thirty (58) _____
thirty-first (94) _____
this (8) _____
those (37) _____
three (22) _____
3D animation (82) _____
throw water (96) _____
Thursday (79) _____
tie [clothing] (106) _____
time (79) _____
time [saying the time] (79) _____
tired (52) _____
to (2) _____
today (5) _____
together (53) _____
tomorrow (9) _____
too (3) _____
town (44) _____
trading card (36) _____
travel (28) _____
tree house (40) _____
T-shirt (36) _____
Tuesday (79) _____
TV (32) _____
TV show (26) _____
TV star (18) _____
twelfth (94) _____
twelve (22) _____
twentieth (94) _____
twenty (22) _____
twenty-eight (58) _____
twenty-eighth (94) _____
twenty-fifth (94) _____
twenty-first (94) _____
twenty-five (58) _____
twenty-four (58) _____
twenty-fourth (94) _____
twenty-nine (58) _____
twenty-ninth (94) _____
twenty-one (58) _____
twenty-second (94) _____
twenty-seven (58) _____
twenty-seventh (94) _____
twenty-six (58) _____
twenty-sixth (94) _____
twenty-third (94) _____
twenty-three (58) _____
twenty-two (58) _____
two (22) _____

Uu
umbrella (30) _____
uncle (58) _____
under (38) _____
uniform (107) _____
United States [the U.S.] (24) _____
used (76) _____
usually (89) _____

Vv
vacation (100) _____
Valentine's Day (92) _____
Venezuela (25) _____
very (37) _____
video arcade (50) _____
video game (32) _____
virtual (40) _____
visit (84) _____
volleyball (52) _____

Ww
wait (73) _____
wall (38) _____
wastebasket (38) _____
watch [noun] (36) _____
waterslide (54) _____
wax (100) _____
we (65) _____
Wednesday (79) _____
weird (33) _____
well (45) _____
what (3) _____
when (93) _____
where (25) _____
white (106) _____
who (17) _____
window (96) _____
wireless (33) _____
with (45) _____
world (28) _____
wow (33) _____
write (65) _____
wrong (53) _____

Yy
yard (66) _____
yeah (53) _____
year (5) _____
yellow (106) _____
yes (5) _____
you (3) _____
youngest (68) _____
your (3) _____

Zz
zero (22) _____
zoo (100) _____

Acknowledgments

Connect, Revised Edition has benefited from extensive development research. The authors and publishers would like to extend their particular thanks to all the CUP editorial, production, and marketing staff, as well as the following reviewers and consultants for their valuable insights and suggestions:

Focus Groups

São Paulo Suzi T. Almeida, Colégio Rio Branco; **Andreia C. Alves**, Colégio Guilherme de Almeida; **Patricia Del Valle**, Colégio I. L. Peretz; **Elaine Elia**, Centro de Educação Caminho Aberto; **Rosemilda L. Falletti**, Colégio Pio XII; **Amy Foot Gomes**, Instituto D. Placidina; **Lilian I. Leventhal**, Colégio I. L. Peretz; **Adriana Pellegrino**, Colégio Santo Agostinho; **Maria de Fátima Sanchez**, Colégio Salesiano Sta. Teresinha; **Regina C. B. Saponara**, Colégio N. S. do Sion; **Neuza C. Senna**, Colégio Henri Wallon; **Camila Toniolo Silva**, Colégio I. L. Peretz; **Izaura Valverde**, Nova Escola.

Curitiba Liana Andrade, Colégio Medianeira; **Bianca S. Borges**, Colégio Bom Jesus; **Rosana Fernandes**, Colégio Bom Jesus; **Cecilia Honorio**, Colégio Medianeira; **Regina Linzmayer**, Colégio Bom Jesus; **Maria Cecília Piccoli**, Colégio N. S. Sion; **Ana L. Z. Pinto**, Colégio Bom Jesus; **Mary C. M. dos Santos**, Colégio Bom Jesus; **Andrea S. M. Souza**, Colégio Bom Jesus; **Juçara M. S. Tadra**, Colégio Bom Jesus.

Rio de Janeiro Alcyrema R. Castro, Colégio N. S. da Assunção; **Renata Frazão**, Colégio Verbo Divino; **Claudia G. Goretti**, Colégio dos Jesuítas; **Letícia Leite**, Colégio Verbo Divino; **Livia Mercuri**, WSA Idiomas; **Marta Moraes**, Colégio São Vicente de Paulo; **Claudia C. Rosa**, Colégio Santa Mônica.

Belo Horizonte Júnia Barcelos, Colégio Santo Agostinho; **Rachel Farias**, Colégio Edna Roriz; **Renato Galil**, Colégio Santo Agostinho; **Katia R. P. A. Lima**, Colégio Santa Maria; **Gleides A. Nonato**, Colégio Arnaldo; **Luciana Queiros**, Instituto Itapoã; **Flávia Samarane**, Colégio Logosófico González Pecotche; **Adriana Zardini**, UFMG.

Brasília José Eugenio F. Alvim, CIL – 01; **Rosemberg Andrade**, Colégio Presbiteriano Mackenzie; **Euzenira Araújo**, CIL – Gama; **Michelle Câmara**, CIL – Gama; **Kátia Falcomer**, Casa Thomas Jefferson; **Almerinda B. Garibaldi**, CIL – Taguatinga; **Michelle Gheller**, CIL – Taguatinga; **Anabel Cervo Lima**, CIL – Brasília; **Ana Lúcia F. de Morais**, CIL – Brazlândia; **Antonio José O. Neto**, CIL – Ceilândia; **Maria da Graça Nóbile**, Colégio Presbiteriano Mackenzie; **Denise A. Nunes**, CIL – Gama; **Suzana Oliveira**, CIL – Taguatinga; **Andréa Pacheco**, Colégio Marista João Paulo II; **Simone Peixoto**, CIL – Brazlândia; **Érica S. Rodrigues**, Colégio Presbiteriano Mackenzie; **Isaura Rodrigues**, CIL – Ceilândia; **Camila Salmazo**, Colégio Marista João Paulo II; **Maria da Guia Santos**, CIL – Gama; **Dóris Scolmeister**, CIL – Gama; **Rejane M. C. de Souza**, Colégio Santa Rosa; **Isabel Teixeira**, CIL – Taguatinga; **Marina Vazquez**, CIL – Gama.

Questionnaires

Brazil Maria Heloísa Alves Audino, Colégio São Teodoro de Nossa Senhora de Sion; **Gleides A. Nonato**, Colégio Amaldo; **Gustavo Henrique Pires**, Instituto Presbiteriano de Educação; **Marta Gabriella Brunale dos Reis**, Colégio Integrado Jaó; **Paula Conti dos Reis Santos**, Colégio Anglo-Latino; **Tânia M. Sasaki**, High Five Language Center.

South Korea Don M. Ahn, EDLS; **Don Bryant**, OnGok Middle School.

Taiwan John A. Davey, Stella Matutina Girls' High School, Taichung City, Taiwan; **Gregory Alan Gwenossis**, Victoria Academy.

Japan Simon Butler, Fujimi Junior and Senior High School; **Yuko Hiroyama**, Pioneer Language School; **Mark Itoh**, Honjo East Senior High School Affiliated Junior High School; **Norio Kawakubo**, Yokohama YMCA ACT; **Michael Lambe**, Kyoto Girls Junior and Senior High School; **John George Lowery**, Dokkyo Junior High School/John G. Lowery School of English; **Jacques Stearn**, American Language School; **Simon Wykamp**, Hiroshima Johoku Junior and Senior High School.

Art Direction, book design, and layout services: A+ Comunicação, São Paulo

Illustration Credits

Ken Batelman 46, 49	**Frank Montagna** 14, 15, 33, 37, 106, 107, 112, 113
Michael Brennan 115	**Rob Schuster** 32, 40, 77, 78, 114, 118, 119, 121
David Coulson 30, 31, 42, 43, 52, 53, 60, 61, 80, 104	**Jeff Shelley** 4, 47, 57
Bruce Day 11, 38, 39, 48, 70	**James Yamasaki** 28, 29
James Elston 7, 20, 58, 118, 122, 123	**Sattu Rodrigues** 36
Larry Jones 66, 72, 73, 87, 90	

Photo Acknowledgements

The authors and publishers acknowledge the following sources of copyright material and are grateful for the permissions granted. While every effort has been made, it has not always been possible to identify the sources of all the material used, or to trace all copyright holders. If any omissions are brought to our notice, we will be happy to include the appropriate acknowledgements on reprinting.

Student's Book

p. 6 (T): ©Westend61/Getty Images; p. 6 (TC): ©Comstock/Stockbyte/Getty Images; p.6 (BC): ©Nicholas Prior/The Image Bank/Getty Images; p.6 (B): ©Fuse/Getty Images; p.10: ©kali9/E+/Getty Images; p.12 (T): ©Colleen Cahill/Design Pics/Design Pics/Corbis; p.12 (C): ©Shmuel Thaler/Photolibrary/Getty Images; p.12 (B): © Adam Burn/Corbis; p.13: ©John Giustina/SuperStock/Corbis; p.16 (C): ©Izabela Habur/iStock/Getty Images Plus; p.18 (1): ©J Carter Rinaldi/FilmMagic/Getty Images; p.18 (2): ©Clive Brunskill/Getty Images; p.18 (3): ©COLUMBIA PICTURES / THE KOBAL COLLECTION; p.18 (4): ©Suhaimi Abdullah/Getty Images; p.18 (5): Christopher Polk/Getty Images for NARAS; p.18 (6): Han Myung-Gu/WireImage; p.18 (7): Mike Coppola/DCNYRE2015/Getty Images for dcp; p.19: ©Bruce Laurence/The Image Bank/Getty Images; p.20 (L): ©Bill Reitzel/Digital Vision/Getty Images; p.20 (C): © Blend

Images/Alamy; p.20 (R): ©Sean De Burca/Corbis; p.21: ©Radius Images/Getty Images Plus; p.22 (TL): ©Jani Bryson/iStock / Getty Images Plus; p.22 (CL): ©arek_malang/Shutterstock; p.22 (BL): ©Denis Kuvaev/Shutterstock; p.22 (TR): ©Hill Street Studios/Nicole Goddard/Blend Images/Getty Images; p.22 (CR): ©Camille Tokerud/The Image Bank/Getty Images; p.22 (BR): ©RedChopsticks/Getty Images; p.23 (L): ©Jupiterimages/Stockbyte/Getty Images; p.23 (CL): ©Monkey Business Images/Shutterstock; p.23 (CR): ©Asia Images Group/Getty Images; p.23 (R): ©michaeljung/Shutterstock; p.24 (BR): ©Barbara Peacock/The Image Bank/Getty Images; p. 24: (tablet and smart phone): ©Youzitx/Getty Images; p.25 (BL): ©hadynyah/E+/Getty Images; p.25 (BCL): ©michaeljung/Shutterstock; p.25 (BCR): ©Vikram Raghuvanshi/iStock / Getty Images Plus; p.25 (BR): ©Vincenzo Lombardo/Stockbyte/Getty Images; p. 25 (background): © roccomontoya/Getty Images; p.26 (TL): ©Chepe Nicoli/Shutterstock; p.26 (CL): Getty Images/Getty Images; p.26(BL): ©George Pimentel/WireImage/Getty Images; p.26 (TR): ©Warner Br/Everett/REX; p.26 (CR): ©Jeffrey Mayer/WireImage/Getty Images; p.26 (BR): ©George Doyle/Stockbyte/Getty Images; p.27: ©Reg Charity/Corbis; p.33 (B): The Asahi Shimbun/Getty Images; p.34 (a): ©CostinT/E+/Getty Images; p.34 (b): ©Valeri Potapova/Shutterstock; p.34 (c): ©GeorgeMPhotography/Shutterstock; p.34 (d): ©domnitsky/Shutterstock; p.34 (e): ©FERNANDO BLANCO CALZADA/Shutterstock; p.34 (f): ©berents/iStock/Getty Images Plus; p.35 (1): ©Michiel de Wit/Shutterstock; p.35 (2): ©Massimiliano Pieraccini/Shutterstock; p.35 (finger repeated 3 times): ©studi-oVin/Shutterstock; p.35 (3): ©i store/Alamy; p.35 (4): ©tankist276/Shutterstock; p.35 (hand): ƒVladislavGudovskiy/Shutterstock; p.35 (5): ©FERNANDO BLANCO CALZADA/Shutterstock; p.35 (6): ©nanD_Phanuwat/Shutterstock; p.36 (1): ©hamurishi/Shutterstock; p.36 (2): ©Mauricio de Sousa Editora Ltda; p.36 (3: bike): ©Ozger Aybike Sarikaya/Shutterstock; p.36 (3: character): ©Warner Br/Everett/REX; p.36 (4): ©Indigo Fish/Shutterstock; p.36 (5): ©Steven May/Alamy; p.36 (6 red): ©FlamingPumpkin/E+/Getty Images; p.36 (6 green): ©Michael Burrell/Alamy; p.40: ©Derek Latta/Photodisc/Getty; p.41: ©Ingram Publishing/Getty Images; p.43: ©Julia Ivantsova/Shutterstock; p.44 (a): ©Directphoto Collection/Alamy; p.44 (b): ©China Photos/Alamy; p.44 (c): ©IMAGEMORE Co.,Ltd./Getty Images; p.44 (d): © Kim Karpeles/Alamy; p.44 (e): ©Jeff Greenberg 2 of 6/Alamy; p.44 (f): ©Adisa/Shutterstock; p.50 (TL): ©David L. Moore/Alamy; p.50 (TR): ©VisitBritain/Doug McKinlay; p.50 (CL): © John James/Alamy; p.50 (CR): ©Tom Hopkins/Aurora/Getty Images; p.50 (BL): ©Rayman/Photographer's Choice RF/Getty Images; p.50 (BR): ©Kevin Britland/Alamy; p.54 (T): ©William Manning/Corbis; p.54 (B): ©Terrance Klassen/Alamy; p.55 (L): ©Sean Justice/The Image Bank/Getty Images; p.55 (R): ©Rob Lewine/Getty Images; p.62 (Jordan): ©Rob Lewine/Getty Images; p.62 (Lori): ©Digitalskillet/iStock / Getty Images Plus; p.62 (Chris): ©Johnny Greig/iStock / Getty Images Plus; p.62 (Jill): ©Samuel Borges Photography/Shutterstock; p.62 (Jerimiah): ©brbimages/E+/Getty Images; p.63 (BL): ©Tom Stewart/Corbis; p.63 (BC): ©StockLite/Shutterstock; p.63 (BR): ©Darama/Corbis; p.64 (1): ©Mitchell Funk/Photographer's Choice/Getty Images; p.64 (2): ©Susan Pease/Alamy; p.64 (3): ©Nancy Hoyt Belcher/Alamy; p.64 (4): Gavin Hellier/Robert Harding World Imagery/Getty Images; p.64 (5): ©Raymond Forbes/age fotostock/Getty Images; p.64 (6): ColorBlind Images/Iconica/Getty Images; p.67 (1): ©romakoma/Shutterstock; p.67 (2): © Mick Roessler/Corbis; p.67 (3): ©Pung/Shutterstock; p.68: ©RonTech200/E+/Getty Images; p.69: © Photo Network/Alamy; p.71: ©George Doyle/Stockbyte/Getty Imafes; p.74 (1): © Kinn Deacon/Alamy; p.74 (2): ©Aerial Archives/Alamy; p.74 (3): ©Steve Collender/Shutterstock; p.74 (4): ©LI CHAOSHU/Shutterstock; p.74 (5): ©Dale May/Corbis; p.74 (6): ©Comstock Images/Stockbyte/Getty Images; p.74 (7): ©Javier Larrea/age fotostock/Getty Images; p.74 (8): ©Jetta Productions/Digital Vision/Getty Images; p.74 (9): ©Baerbel Schmidt/Stone/Getty Images; p.76 (TL): ©nevodka/Shutterstock; p.76 (TR): ©Jamie Grill/Iconica/Getty Images; p.76 (CR): ©Hurst Photo/Shutterstock ; p.76 (BL): ©Tomasz Trojanowski/Shutterstock ; p.76 (BR): ©photogl/Shutterstock; p.82 (T): © Hero Images Inc./Hero Images Inc./Corbis; p.82 (C): © Hero Images/Corbis; p.82 (B): ©Larry Dle Gordon/The Image Bank/Getty Images; p.83: ©Goodshot/Getty Images Plus/Getty Images; p.84 (T): ©SNEHIT/Shutterstock; p.84 (B): Dennis O'Clair/The Image Bank/Getty Images; p.85 (TL): ©dwphotos/Shutterstock; p.85 (TR): ©Umberto Shtanzman/Shutterstock; p.85 (BL): ©Maria Dryfhout/Shutterstock; p.85 (BR): ©Zadorozhnyi Viktor/Shutterstock; p.88 (TL): ©Lawrence Lucier/FilmMagic/Getty Images; p.88 (TR): ©Jason Miller/Getty Images; p.88 (BL): ©Steve Babineau/NBAE via Getty Images; p.88 (BR): ©Dave J Hogan/Getty Images; p.89 (T): ©Mireya Acierto/Getty Images; p.89 (B): ©GONZALO/Bauer-Griffin/GC Images; p.92 (1): ©Andrew Olney/Digital Vision/Getty Images; p.92 (2): ©Zadorozhnyi Viktor/Shutterstock; p.92 (3): ©Jose Luis Pelaez Inc/Blend Images/Getty Images; p.92 (4): © Ingram Publishing/Alamy; p.92 (5): ©Richard Levine/Alamy; p.92 (6): © Pontino/Alamy; p.93 (T): © F1online digitale Bildagentur GmbH / Alamy; p.93 (B): ©Richard Levine/Alamy; p.95 (TL): ©Rob Lewine/Getty Images; p.95 (TR): ©Radius Images/Getty Images; p.95 (BR): ©Romiana Lee/Shutterstock; p.96: ©Timothy A. Clary/AFP/Getty Images; p.97: ©B2M Productions/Photographer's Choice RF/Getty Images; p.98 (L): ©Koichi Kamoshida/Getty Images; p.98 (TC): Frazer Harrison/Getty Images for 102.7 KIIS FM's Wango Tango; p.98 (TR): Clemens Bilan/Getty Images; p.98 (BL): Jemal Countess/Getty Images; p.98 (BR):©Jamie McCarthy/WireImage; p.100 (L): ©Tyler Boyes/Shutterstock; p.100 (C): ©npine/Shutterstock; p.100 (R): © Rodolfo Arpia/Alamy; p.101 (T): © F1online digitale Bildagentur GmbH / Alamy; p.101 (C): JTB/UIG via Getty Images; p.101 (B): ©Image Source/Getty Images; p.102 (TL): ©Sean Justice/The Image Bank/Getty Images; p.102 (TC): ©Steven May/Alamy; p.102 (TR): ©Andersen Ross/Stockbyte/Getty Images; p.102 (BL): ©Ned Frisk/Corbis; p.102 (BC): ©James Darell/Digital Vision/Getty Images; p.102 (BR): ©Windzepher/iStock/Getty Images Plus; p. 105 (TL): ©David R. Frazier Photolibrary, Inc./Alamy; p. 105 (TC): ©Peter Gridley/Stockbyte/Getty Images; p. 105 (TR): ©Fraser Hall/Photographer's Choice RF/Getty Images; p. 105 (BL): ©Chad Slattery/The Image Bank/Getty Images; p. 105 (BC): ©ShootingCompany/Alamy; p. 105(BR): ©Fuse/Getty Images; p.108 (1): ©Jose Luis Pelaez Inc/Blend Images/Getty Images; p.108 (2): ©LWA/Dann Tardif/Blend Images/Getty Images; p.108 (3): ©Corbis; p.108 (4): ©altrendo images/Getty Images; p.108 (5): ©Ant Strack/Corbis; p.108 (6): ©JeffreyIsaacGreenberg/Alamy; p.108 (7): ©Andersen Ross/The Image Bank/Getty Images; p.108 (8): ©Jennifer Boggs/Photolibrary/Getty Images; p.110: ©Richard Levine/Alamy; p.111: ©Image Source/Getty Images; p.116 (1): ©Aaron Amat/Shutterstock; p.116 (2): ©SAIndor Kelemen/iStock / Getty Images Plus; p.116 (3): ©Gyvafoto/Shutterstock; p.116 (4): ©Oleksiy Mark/iStock / Getty Images Plus; p.116 (5): ©Siede Preis/Photodisc/Getty Images; p.116 (6): ©Theerapol Pongkangsananan/Shutterstock; p.116 (7): ©Everything/Shutterstock; p.116 (8): ©Chiyacat/Shutterstock; p.116 (9): ©Gayvoronskaya_Yana/Shutterstock; p.116 (10): ©MarkHededus/iStock / Getty Images Plus; p.116 (11): ©Konjushenko Vladimir/Shutterstock; p.116 (12): ©Robnroll/Shutterstock; p.120 (1): Corbis; p.120 (2): ©Jorg Hackemann/Shutterstock; p.120 (3): ©Leslie Richard Jacobs/Corbis; p.120 (4): ©Dafinka/Shutterstock; p.120 (5): ©Justin Atkins/Shutterstock; p.120 (6): isitsharp/Vetta/Getty Images; p.120 (7): ©Owen Franken/CORBIS; p.120 (8): ©Otto Rogge/CORBIS; p.125: ©dbimages/Alamy; p.126 (T): ©Rick Gomez/Blend Images/Corbis; p.126 (BL): ©Bloomimage/Corbis; p.126 (BCL): ©Comstock/Stockbyte/Getty Images; p.126 (BCR): ©jaroon/

iStock/Getty Images Plus; p.126 (BR): ©Samuel Borges Photography/Shutterstock; p.127 (T): ©Stockbyte/Getty Images; p.127 (C): ©Juanmonino/iStock/Getty Images Plus/Getty Images; p.127 (B): ©Mark Bowden/E+/Getty Images; p.128 (TR): ©LdF/E+/Getty Images; p.128 (TC): Oleksiy Mark/iStock / Getty Images Plus; p.128 (TL): ©SA!ndor Kelemen/iStock / Getty Images Plus; p.128 (TV): ©Piotr Adamowicz/Shutterstock; p.128 (game): ©forest_strider/iStock / Getty Images Plus; p.128 (MP3): ©trucic/Shutterstock; P.128 (clock): ©Crisp/Shutterstock; p.128 (computer): ©scanrail/iStock / Getty Images Plus; p.129 (TL): © Mathias Beinling / Alamy; p.129 (TR): © Kim Karpeles / Alamy; p.129 (C): © Emily Riddell/Alamy; p.129 (B): © Robert Harding World Imagery / Alamy; p.130 (T): © Rob Lewine/Tetra Images/Corbis; p.130 (B): ©Daniel M Ernst/Shutterstock; p.131 (TL): ©charistoone-travel/Alamy; p.131 (TR): © Jim West/Alamy; p.131 (media centre): © dpa picture alliance / Alamy; p.131 (football): © PCN Photography / Alamy; p.131 (swim): ©with-God/Shutterstock; p.132 (T): ©Johnny Greig/Alamy; p.132 (CL): ©SeanPavonePhoto/iStock / Getty Images Plus; p.132 (CR): ©John W Banagan/Photographer's Choice/Getty Images; p.132 (B): © Kim Kyung-Hoon/Reuters/Corbis; p. 133 (TL): ©Preto Perola/Shutterstock; p.133 (TR): ©hamurishi/Shutterstock

Commissioned photography by Lawrence Migdale for pages 2, 3, 5 (T & B), 8 (TL, TR, BL & BR), 9, 16 (TL, TR, BL, CR & BR), 17, 24 (L, TC, TR & BC), 25 (TL, TCL, TCR & TR), 33 (T), 36 (TL, BR); 45 (L & R), 51, 63 (T), 64 (7 & 8), 75, 79, 81, 91, 94, 103, 109 (L & R).

Cover photograph by Joe McBride/Getty Images.

Art Direction, book design, and layout services: A+ Comunicação, São Paulo

revised edition

Connect

**Jack C. Richards
Carlos Barbisan**
com Chuck Sandy e
Dorothy E. Zemach

Combo 1
Workbook

CAMBRIDGE
UNIVERSITY PRESS

Table of Contents

Unit 1 Back to School
Lesson 1   Classmates 2
Lesson 2   Hello. 3
Mini-review 4
Lesson 3   After school 5
Lesson 4   Names 6
Get Connected 7
Check Yourself 8

Unit 2 Favorite People
Lesson 5   Teachers and friends 9
Lesson 6   Favorite stars 10
Mini-review 11
Lesson 7   Birthdays 12
Lesson 8   E-pals 13
Get Connected 14
Check Yourself 15

Unit 3 Everyday Things
Lesson 9   What a mess! 16
Lesson 10 Cool things 17
Mini-review 18
Lesson 11 Favorite things 19
Lesson 12 Where is it? 20
Get Connected 21
Check Yourself 22

Unit 4 Around Town
Lesson 13 At the movies 23
Lesson 14 Downtown 24
Mini-review 25
Lesson 15 At the mall 26
Lesson 16 Any suggestions? 27
Get Connected 28
Check Yourself 29

Unit 5 Family and Home
Lesson 17 My family 30
Lesson 18 Family reunion 31
Mini-review 32
Lesson 19 My new city 33
Lesson 20 At home 34
Get Connected 35
Check Yourself 36

Unit 6 At School
Lesson 21 The media center 37
Lesson 22 Around school 38
Mini-review 39
Lesson 23 School subjects 40
Lesson 24 Spring Day 41
Get Connected 42
Check Yourself 43

Unit 7 Around the World
Lesson 25 People and countries 44
Lesson 26 Nationalities 45
Mini-review 46
Lesson 27 Holidays 47
Lesson 28 Important days 48
Get Connected 49
Check Yourself 50

Unit 8 Teen Time
Lesson 29 Favorite places 51
Lesson 30 Talent show 52
Mini-review 53
Lesson 31 School fashion 54
Lesson 32 Teen tastes 55
Get Connected 56
Check Yourself 57

Lesson 1: Classmates

1 Number the sentences in the correct order.

___ Nice to meet you, Ana.
___ My name is Ana.
_1_ Hi. I'm Valerie. What's your name?
___ Nice to meet you, too.

2 Choose the correct words to complete the conversation.

A Hello. My name is Koji.
   What's (Is / What's) your name?

B Hi, Koji. _____ (I'm / My) Joanie.
   Nice to meet you.

A Nice to meet _____ (you / your), too.

3 Introduce yourself to Jake. Complete the conversation.

Hi. My name is Jake. What's your name?

_____

Nice to meet you.

_____

UNIT 1 Back to School

Lesson 2 — Hello.

1 Look at the pictures. Complete the conversations with the sentences in the box.

☐ Fine, thank you.   ☐ Good morning.   ☑ How are you today?
☐ Good evening.   ☐ How about you?   ☐ Not too good.

1. A Good afternoon, Suzy.
   B _How are you today?_
   A _____
   B Great!

2. A _____
      How are you?
   B Not bad, thanks.
      _____
   A Good.

3. A _____
   B Hello, Mr. Gomez. How are you?
   A _____

2 Choose the correct titles.

1. I'm _Miss_ (Miss / Mrs.) Johnson. I'm single.

2. My name is _____ (Ms. / Miss) Morales. I'm married.

3. I'm _____ (Mrs. / Mr.) Weston. I'm married.

4. My name is _____ (Mrs. / Ms.) Lee. I'm single.

Back to School 3

Lessons 1 & 2 Mini-review

1 Complete the conversations with the words in the box.

☐ are ☑ hi ☐ meet ☐ nice ☐ thanks
☐ hello ☐ how ☐ my ☐ not ☐ your

1. A ____Hi____ . I'm Eva. What's _____ name?

   B _____ name is Matt.

   A _____ to meet you, Matt.

   B Nice to _____ you, too.

2. A Hi, Miss Valdes.

   B _____ , Corey. How _____ you today?

   A _____ bad. _____ about you?

   B Great, _____ .

2 Rewrite the sentences. Correct the underlined words.

1. <u>Bad</u> to meet you, Lydia.

   Nice to meet you, Lydia.

2. Hi. I'm Mrs. Martinez. What's your <u>afternoon</u>?

   _____

3. Hi. My <u>hello</u> is Robert.

   _____

4. <u>What's</u> are you today?

   _____

5. I'm not bad. How about <u>your</u>?

   _____

6. <u>OK</u> afternoon, Mrs. Lyon.

   _____

7. <u>Good</u> I'm late, Mr. Morgan.

   _____

4 Unit 1

Lesson 3: After school

1 Choose the correct words to complete the conversations.

1. A _Hi_ (Hi / Bye), Carla.
   B Hello, Rose. This _____ (is / are) Doug Jones.
   A Nice to _____ (see / meet) you, Doug.

2. A _____ (Good-bye / Hello), Tom.
   B See you _____ (late / later), Mr. Shields.

3. A _____ (Good-bye / Good evening), Ms. Cooper. How are you?
   B I'm good, _____ (thank / thanks).

4. A Sarah, _____ (you / this) is Ms. Nelson.
   Ms. Nelson, _____ (you / this) is Sarah Finnegan.
   B Nice to meet _____ (you / your), Ms. Nelson.
   C Nice to meet you, _____ (you / too), Sarah.

2 Match the pictures to the conversations in Part 1.

a.

b.

c.

d.

3 Write the correct responses.

1. Gisele, this is Pedro.
   _____

2. Nice to meet you.
   _____

3. How are you today?
   _____

4. See you tomorrow.
   _____

Back to School 5

Lesson 4 — Names

1 Look at the pictures. Complete the forms for the students.

1.  First Name: Leticia
   Last Name: Webber

2.  First Name: _____
   Last Name: _____

3.  First Name: _____
   Last Name: _____

4.  First Name: _____
   Last Name: _____

2 Match the questions to the answers.

1. Hello. How are you today? _d_
2. What's your name? ___
3. How do you spell your first name? ___
4. And how do you spell your last name? ___

a. Leticia Webber.
b. L-E-T-I-C-I-A.
c. W-E-B-B-E-R.
d. Good, thanks.

3 Complete the conversation in Part 2 with your own information.

A Hello. How are you today?
You _____
A What's your name?
You _____
A _____
You _____
A _____
You _____

6 Unit 1

UNIT 1 Get Connected

1 Read the conversation quickly. Write the first names of the two people.

1. _____   2. _____

www.doglovers.gc

I like dogs.

JK110: Hi. I'm Joshua Kemp. My <u>nickname</u> is Josh. What's your name?

GSdog: My <u>name</u> is Gabriela Silva. My nickname is Gabi. Nice to meet you.

JK110: Nice to meet you, too. How are you?

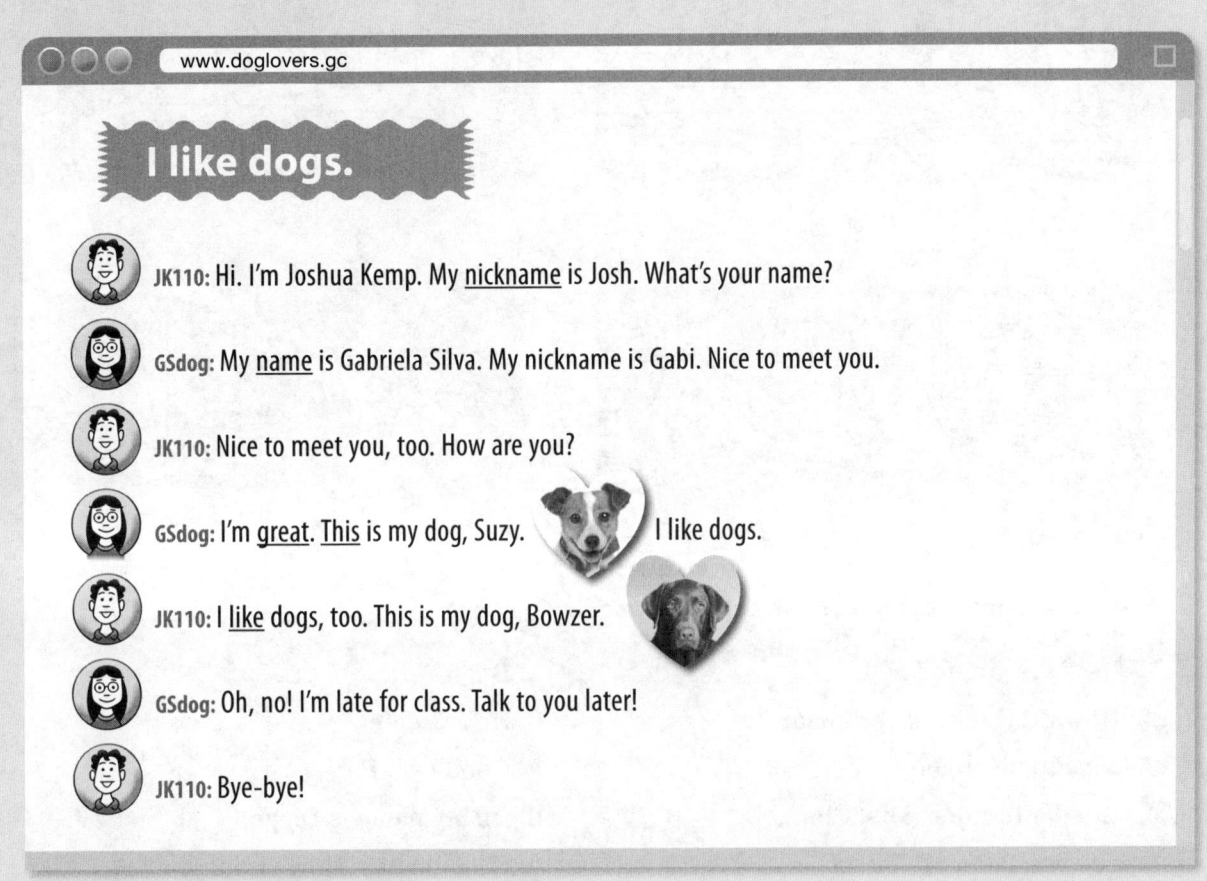

GSdog: I'm <u>great</u>. <u>This</u> is my dog, Suzy.   I like dogs.

JK110: I <u>like</u> dogs, too. This is my dog, Bowzer.

GSdog: Oh, no! I'm late for class. Talk to you later!

JK110: Bye-bye!

2 Complete the sentences. Use the underlined words in the conversation in Part 1.

1. My first name is Madison. My <u>nickname</u> is Maddy.
2. I _____ music.
3. _____ is my dog, Lucky.
4. My last _____ is Levinson.
5. I'm _____ . How are you?

3 Read the conversation in Part 1 slowly. Complete the chart.

First name	Last name	Nickname	Dog's name
	Kemp		
		Gabi	

Back to School 7

UNIT 1 Check Yourself

1 Label the pictures with the sentences in the box.

☐ Good afternoon.   ☐ Good evening.   ☐ Good morning.   ☐ Good night.

1. _____   2. _____

3. _____   4. _____

2 Match the sentences to the correct responses.

1. How are you today? ____
2. How do you spell your name? ____
3. Nice to meet you. ____
4. Good afternoon, Mrs. Chu. ____
5. See you later, Mr. Simon. ____
6. My name is Grace. ____

a. B-R-Y-A-N.
b. Hi, Jasmine.
c. Good-bye, Pete.
d. Hi. My name is Diego.
e. Fine, thanks. How about you?
f. Nice to meet you, too.

3 Complete the conversations.

1. **Janet** Hi! _____ name is Janet. What's _____ name?

   Sandy _____ Sandy. Nice to meet _____ .

2. **Lisa** _____ are you today, Mrs. Martinez?

   Mrs. Martinez Not _____ , thank you. How _____ you?

   Lisa I'm great.

3. **Mr. Cohen** _____ morning, Taro.

   Taro _____ I'm late, Mr. Cohen.

8   Check Yourself

Lesson 5: Teachers and friends

1 Who are the people in Cindy's life? Write two sentences for each number.

1. This is my computer lab partner.
   His name is Jack.
   This is my computer lab partner, Jack.
   Jack is my computer lab partner.

2. This is my best friend.
   Her name is Laura.
   _____
   _____

3. This is my math teacher.
   His name is Mr. Larson.
   _____
   _____

4. This is my classmate.
   Her name is Maggie.
   _____
   _____

2 Complete the conversations with *What's his name?*, *What's her name?*, or *Who's this?*

1. A   *Who's this?*
   B   My classmate.

2. A   _____
   B   Her name is Emily.

3. A   _____
   B   This is my friend, Larry.

4. A   _____
   B   His name is Mr. Fuller.

5. A   _____
   B   My coach.

6. A   _____
   B   Her name is Ms. Patterson.

UNIT 2 Favorite People

Favorite People   9

Lesson 6: Favorite stars

1 Complete the chart with the words in the box.

- ☑ actor
- ☐ cartoon character
- ☐ English teacher
- ☐ singer
- ☐ basketball coach
- ☐ classmate
- ☐ model
- ☐ TV star
- ☐ best friend
- ☐ computer partner

People at school	Stars
	actor

2 Match the pictures to the sentences. Then write sentences with the words from the Stars column in Part 1.

1.  a. This is Josh Hartnett.
   He's my favorite actor.

2. b. This is Gru.

3. c. This is Ryan Seacrest.

   a

4. d. This is Tyson Beckford.

5. e. This is Alicia Keys.

Lessons 5 & 6 Mini-review

1 Choose the correct responses.

1. 
   A What's her name?
   B _Her name is Dina._
   ☐ I'm Lisa.
   ☑ Her name is Dina.

2. 
   A Who's this?
   B _____
   ☐ His English teacher is Mrs. Kramer.
   ☐ My best friend.

3. 
   A Who's your favorite actor?
   B _____
   ☐ Johnny Depp.
   ☐ He's my classmate.

4. 
   A What's her name?
   B _____
   ☐ Her name is Jenny.
   ☐ She's my tennis partner.

2 Complete the questions with the words in the box. Then answer the questions with your own information.

☐ best   ☑ English   ☐ last   ☐ TV

1. **Q:** Who's your _English_ teacher?
   A: _____
2. **Q:** Who's your favorite _____ star?
   A: _____
3. **Q:** What's your _____ name?
   A: _____
4. **Q:** Who's your _____ friend?
   A: _____

3 Who are your favorite stars? Complete the chart with your own information.

Star	Name	Sentence
1. model	Gisele Bündchen	She's my favorite model.
2. singer		
3. TV star		
4. actor		
5. cartoon character		

Favorite People 11

Lesson 7 Birthdays

1 Write the numbers.

1. (7) _seven_
2. (18) _____
3. (20) _____
4. (6) _____
5. (12) _____
6. (3) _____
7. (19) _____
8. (11) _____
9. (4) _____
10. (16) _____
11. (8) _____
12. (1) _____

2 Circle the correct words to complete the conversation.

A Hi. My name's Carlos.
B (Good night / (Hello)). My name's John.
A (How / What) old (is / are) you?
B (You're / I'm) thirteen.
A (Who / How) about (your / my) little sister? (Is / Are) she six?
B (She's / He's) not (five / six). (She's / He's) four.

3 Write questions. Use the information in the chart.

	Louisa	Jeff	Keiko	Pedro
11	✓			
12				✓
13			✓	
14		✓		

1. **Q:** _How old is Jeff?_
   A: He's fourteen.
2. **Q:** _____
   A: She's eleven.
3. **Q:** _____
   A: He's twelve.
4. **Q:** _____
   A: She's thirteen.

4 Correct the sentences. Use the information in the chart in Part 3.

1. Pedro is eleven.
   Pedro is twelve.
2. Jeff is twelve.
   _____
3. Louisa is seventeen.
   _____
4. Keiko is ten.
   _____

12   Unit 2

Lesson 8: E-pals

1 Match the questions to the answers.

1. Where are you from? ____
2. Where's John from? ____
3. Marisa's from Peru, right? ____
4. You're from Japan, right? ____
5. Where's she from? ____
6. He's from Portugal, right? ____

a. She's not from Peru. She's from Colombia.
b. I'm from Mexico.
c. I'm not from Japan. I'm from China.
d. He's from France.
e. He's not from Portugal. He's from Canada.
f. She's from the U.S.

2 Write questions and answers.

1. she? / Australia
   A *Where's she from?*
   B *She's from Australia.*

2. he? / Colombia
   A _____
   B _____

3. she from Mexico, right? / from Brazil
   A _____
   B _____

4. he from Canada, right? / from the U.S.
   A _____
   B _____

5. you? / Brazil
   A _____
   B _____

6. she? / Venezuela
   A _____
   B _____

7. you from Peru, right? / from Colombia
   A _____
   B _____

8. he? / Portugal
   A _____
   B _____

Favorite People

UNIT 2   Get Connected

1 Read the article quickly. Underline the names and nicknames of the coach and the best friend.

My Coach and My Friend

This is my basketball coach, Ms. Rider. She's my science teacher, too. Her nickname is Coach R. Her favorite sports are basketball, soccer, and tennis. She's not from the U.S. She's from Canada. I think she's really funny. She's my favorite teacher. And she's my favorite coach, too!

Here's a photo of my best friend, Rafael. His nickname is Rafi. He's not from the U.S. He's from Peru. His favorite TV show is *CSI*. His favorite TV star is Ashton Kutcher. He likes music. His favorite singer is Chris Daughtry.

2 Match the words to the meanings.

1. Peru _b_
2. science ___
3. *CSI* ___
4. Chris Daughtry ___
5. tennis ___
6. Ashton Kutcher ___

a. a sport
b. a country
c. a school subject
d. a TV star
e. a TV show
f. a singer

3 Read the article in Part 1 slowly. Circle the words to complete the sentences.

1. Ms. Rider is a ((basketball) / soccer) coach.
2. She's a (star / science) teacher.
3. Her (last name / nickname) is Coach R.
4. Rafael is not from (the U.S. / Peru).
5. He likes (music / soccer).
6. His favorite (singer / TV star) is Ashton Kutcher.

UNIT 2 Check Yourself

1 Label the pictures with the words in the box.

```
☐ actor          ☐ best friend        ☐ model    ☑ soccer coach
☐ basketball player ☐ cartoon character ☐ singer  ☐ teacher
```

1. _soccer coach_
2. _____
3. _____
4. _____
5. _____
6. _____
7. _____
8. _____

2 Write questions.

1. **Q:** _____
   A: I'm eleven.

2. **Q:** _____
   A: She's from Brazil.

3. **Q:** _____
   A: My name is Jeremy.

4. **Q:** _____
   A: He's my science teacher.

5. **Q:** _____
   A: His name is Charlie.

6. **Q:** _____
   A: She's not fifteen. She's seventeen.

3 Choose the correct words to complete the paragraphs.

1. I'm Jack. This is my favorite __cartoon character__
   (cartoon character / soccer player). _____ (His / Her)
   name is Alex, and _____ (he's / his) from Africa.
   _____ (I'm / I'm not) from Africa. I'm from Australia.
   _____ (My / I'm) fifteen. Alex is not fifteen.
   (She's / He's) _____ an adult.

2. I'm Jamie. This is my favorite tennis player.
   _____ (He's / She's) from Spain. _____ (Her / His)
   name is Rafael Nadal. _____ (I'm / He's) from the U.S.
   _____ (I'm not / I'm) from Canada.

Check Yourself   15

Lesson 9 — What a mess!

1 Check (✓) the items you have in your bag, backpack, or desk.

☐ brush   ☐ notebook
☐ camera ☐ pen
☐ eraser ☐ pencil case
☐ hat   ☐ umbrella

2 Write sentences with *This is* or *That's*.

1. (Amy) _This is Amy's backpack._
2. (Nick) _____ 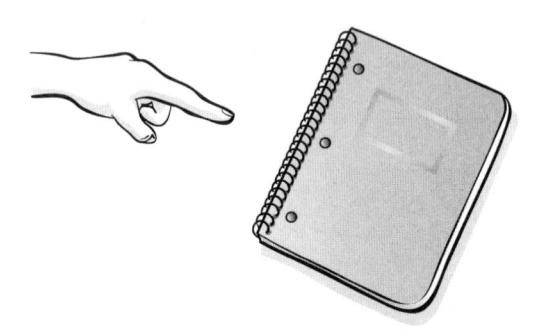
3. (Ricardo) _____ 
4. (John) _____ 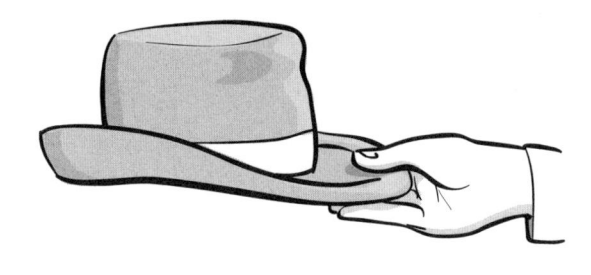
5. (Brad) _____ 
6. (Erica) _____ 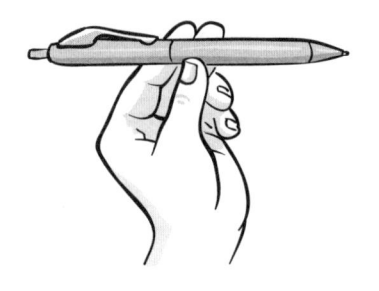
7. (Ken) _____ 
8. (Viviana) _____ 

UNIT 3 Everyday Things

16

Lesson 10 Cool things

1 Write questions. Then write *a* or *an* to complete the answers.

1. Marc _What's that?_
   Jacki It's _a_ video game.

2. Marc _____
   Jacki It's ____ alarm clock.

3. Jacki _____
   Marc It's ____ MP3 player.

4. Marc _____
   Jacki It's ____ cell phone.

5. Marc _____
   Jacki It's ____ laptop.

6. Jacki _____
   Marc It's ____ umbrella.

2 Number the sentences in the correct order.

1. ___ It's a video game.
   ___ No, it's not. It's a TV.
   ___ Hmm. It's weird. And what's that?
   ___ Wow! It's really cool!
   _1_ Maria, what's this? A desktop computer?

2. ___ No, it's a cell phone. It's a calculator, too.
   ___ It's an MP3 player.
   _1_ What's that, Robby?
   ___ Wow! It's really great.
   ___ Really? It's weird. And what's this? A video game?

Everyday Things 17

Lessons 9 & 10 Mini-review

1 What does Kerri say about her things? Write sentences.

1. *That's my cell phone.*
2. _____
3. _____
4. _____
5. _____
6. _____
7. _____
8. _____

2 Circle the correct words to complete the conversation.

Mr. Simms: Good morning. This is your bag, right?

Kerri: Yes. This is (**my** / your) bag.

Mr. Simms: (Who's / What's) this?

Kerri: It's (a / an) alarm clock.

Mr. Simms: Really?

Kerri: Yes. It's (a / an) MP3 player, too.

Mr. Simms: I see. What's (it / that)?

Kerri: Oh, it's (a / an) calculator.

3 Check (✓) the correct responses.

1. What's this?
   - ✓ It's a notebook.
   - ☐ Hmm. It's weird.

2. What's that?
   - ☐ Really? It's great!
   - ☐ It's an address book.

3. And what's that?
   - ☐ That's Christina's pen.
   - ☐ Wow! It's really cool.

4. Hey, Carlos. What's this?
   - ☐ What's that? A laptop?
   - ☐ It's Molly's laptop.

18 Unit 3

Lesson 11 — Favorite things

1 Complete the puzzle. What's the mystery word?

	¹B	I	C	Y	C	L	E		
			²		D		G		D
			³C						
⁴		O			R				
⁵T		S							
			⁶			C			

2 Complete the conversation with *these*, *those*, or *they're*.

Mateo   What are ___these___ ?
Chris   _____ my favorite trading cards.
Mateo   _____ cool! What are _____ ?
Chris   _____ are my new T-shirts.
Mateo   _____ nice!

3 Complete the conversations with the sentences in the box.

☐ Hmm. They're very interesting.   ☑ Those are my favorite comic books.
☐ These are my posters.   ☐ What are these?

1. A   What are those?
   B   *Those are my favorite comic books.*

2. A   _____
   B   They're my trading cards.

3. A   Those are my favorite video games.
   B   _____

4. A   _____
   B   Oh, they're nice.

Everyday Things 19

Lesson 12 — Where is it?

1 Look at the picture. Write questions and answers.

1. **Q:** <u>Where's the umbrella?</u>
   A: It's next to the dresser.

2. **Q:** _____
   A: They're on the bed.

3. **Q:** _____
   A: It's in the wastebasket.

4. **Q:** Where are the T-shirts?
   A: _____

5. **Q:** Where's the bag?
   A: _____

6. **Q:** Where are the comic books?
   A: _____

2 Choose the correct words to complete the conversation.

Danny Mom! I'm late. __Where's__ (Where's / Where are) my soccer ball?

Mom _____ (It's / They're) under your bed.

Danny OK, but _____ (where's / where are) my books? _____ (It's not / They're not) on my desk.

Mom _____ (It's / They're) on your dresser.

Danny Oh, right. Thanks. And _____ (where's / where are) my calculator? _____ (It's not / They're not) in my bag.

Mom _____ (It's / They're) on your desk.

UNIT 3 Get Connected

1 Read the blog quickly. Circle the correct answers.

1. Penny is a (teenager / cat).   2. Stella is a (spider / cat).   3. Stella likes (spiders / cats).

www.stellasroom.gc

A Teenager's Bedroom

Hi, I'm Penny. This is my virtual bedroom. It's a mess! My laptop is under the bed. My cat is in my backpack. Her name is Stella. There's a spider on the chair! Stella likes spiders.

Where's my watch? It's in the wastebasket! Where are my T-shirts? They're next to the bed. What a mess!

2 Write sentences about the pictures.

1. *The cat is under the desk.*

2. _____

3. _____

4. _____

5. _____

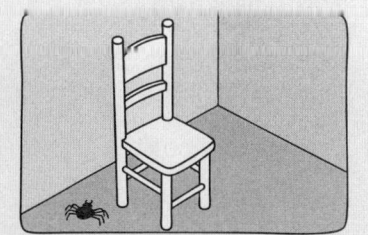

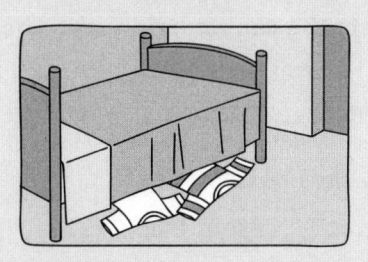

3 Read the blog in Part 1 slowly. Look at the sentences in Part 2. Make them true for Part 1.

1. *The laptop is under the bed.*
2. _____
3. _____
4. _____
5. _____

Everyday Things   21

UNIT 3 Check Yourself

1 Complete the sentences with *a*, *an*, or *the*.

1. What's this? It's __a__ cell phone.
2. That's _____ MP3 player.
3. My books are on _____ laptop.
4. It's _____ alarm clock. It's weird.
5. Jim's bag is next to _____ chair.
6. A What's that? _____ video game?
   B No, it isn't. It's _____ calculator.

2 Look at the picture. Whose things are these? Write Jay's sentences. Begin with *That's*, *This is*, *These are*, or *Those are*.

1. (watch) _This is my watch._
2. (pens) _Those are Cara's pens._
3. (bicycle) _____
4. (pencil case) _____
5. (backpack) _____
6. (comic books) _____
7. (erasers) _____
8. (notebook) _____
9. (hat) _____
10. (pencils) _____
11. (cell phone) _____

3 Look at the picture. Complete the conversation with the words in the box.

☐ in ☐ next to ☐ on ☐ under ☑ where are ☐ where's

Leo — _Where are_ my books?
Mrs. Rivera — They're _____ your bag.
Leo — OK, but _____ my bag?
Mrs. Rivera — It's _____ your desk.
Leo — Where is my camera?
Mrs. Rivera — It's _____ your desk.
Leo — Thanks. Oh! Where's my basketball?
Mrs. Rivera — It's _____ your chair, Leo!

Lesson 13 At the movies

1 Look at the picture. Are the statements true or false? Check (✓) True or False.

	True	False		True	False
1. Linda is at the movie theater.	✓	☐	4. Greg is at the bank.	☐	☐
2. Paul is at the shoe store.	☐	☐	5. Dave is at the shoe store.	☐	☐
3. Aya is at the subway station.	☐	☐	6. Jane is at the Internet café.	☐	☐

2 Number the sentences in the correct order.

____ No, I'm not at the theater. I'm at the bus stop.

____ Well, please hurry. You're late!

__1__ Hi, Carlos. Are you still at home?

____ OK. I'm sorry.

____ No, I'm not.

____ Are you at the movie theater?

3 Complete the conversations.

1. A _Are you_ 12?
   B No, I'm not. I'm 11.

2. A _____ Mexico City?
   B No, I'm not. I'm from Barcelona.

3. A _____ soccer player?
   B Yes, I am. It's my favorite sport.

4. A _____ Salma Hayek fan?
   B Yes, I am. She's my favorite star.

Around Town 23

Lesson 14 Downtown

1 Look at the picture. Write sentences with the words in the box.

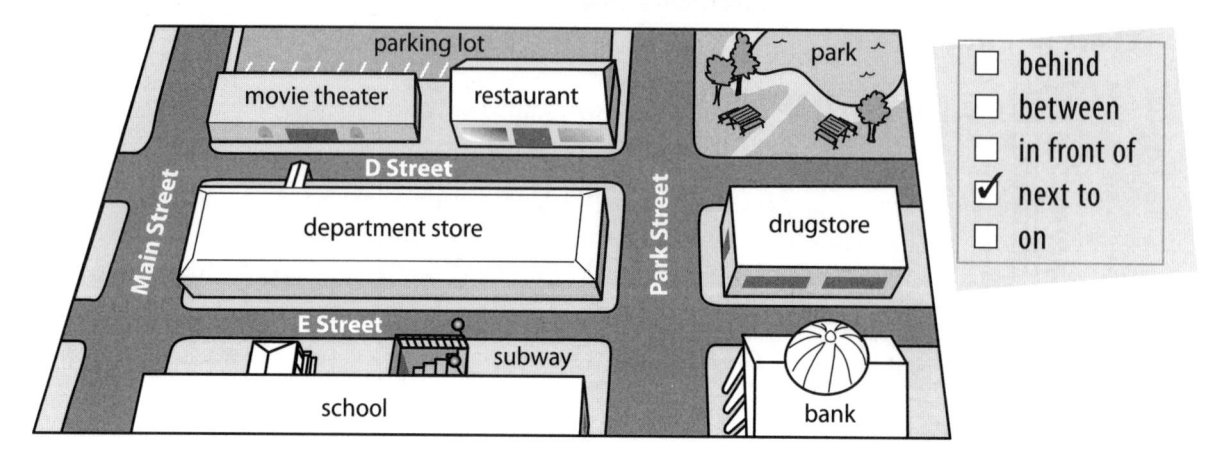

- ☐ behind
- ☐ between
- ☐ in front of
- ☑ next to
- ☐ on

1. (movie theater / restaurant)

   The movie theater is next to the restaurant.

2. (parking lot / movie theater and restaurant)

3. (department store / D Street)

4. (subway station / school)

5. (drugstore / park / bank)

2 Look at the picture in Part 1. Answer the questions. If the answer is *no*, give the correct information.

1. Is the movie theater on E Street?

   No, it's not. It's on D Street.

2. Is the department store next to the movie theater?

3. Is the drugstore between the bank and the department store?

4. Is the restaurant across from the department store?

5. Is the parking lot behind the movie theater?

24   Unit 4

Lessons 13 & 14 Mini-review

1 Check (✓) the correct responses.

1. Are you at home?
   - ✓ Yes, I am. I'm in my room.
   - ☐ Yes, it is. It's on Oak Street.

2. Is your school next to a park?
   - ☐ Yes, I am. I'm at school.
   - ☐ No, it isn't. It's across from a park.

3. Are you from Brazil?
   - ☐ Yes, I am. I'm a soccer fan.
   - ☐ No, I'm not. I'm from Peru.

4. Are you 13?
   - ☐ No, I'm not. I'm 14.
   - ☐ Yes, I'm still at the basketball game.

2 Answer the questions in Part 1 with your own information.

1. _____
2. _____
3. _____
4. _____

3 Look at the picture. Then circle the correct words to complete the sentences.

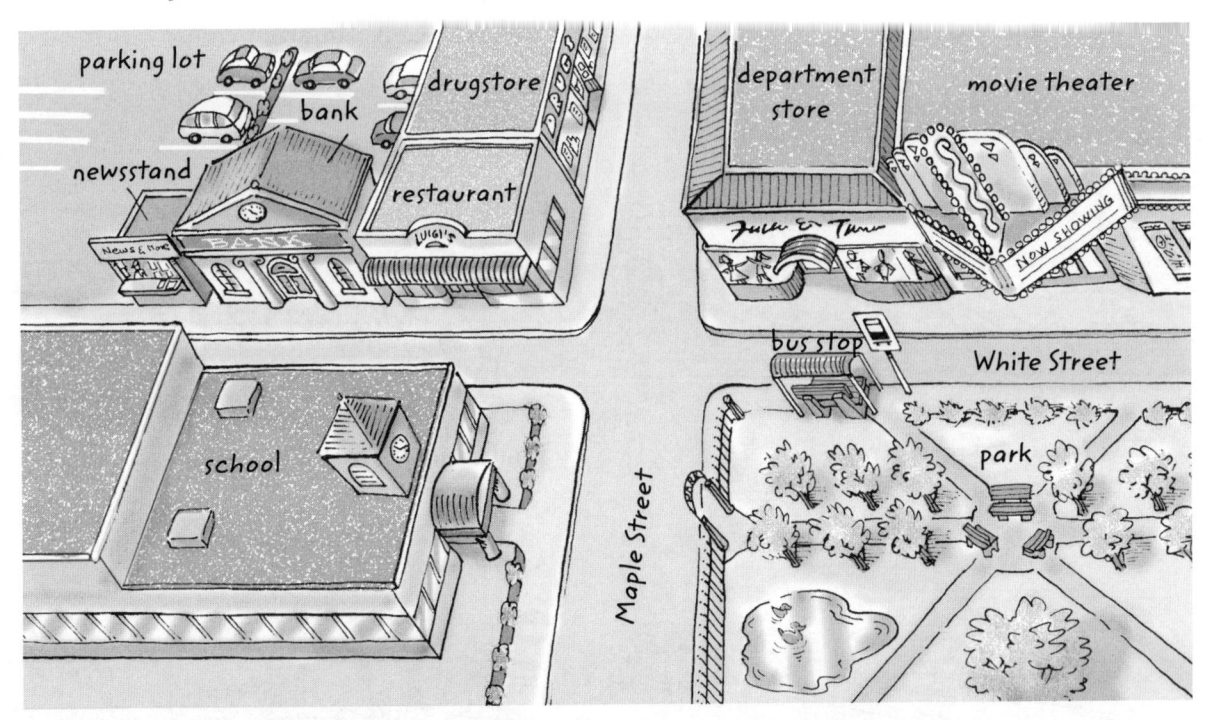

1. The bank is ((between) / in front of) the newsstand and the restaurant.
2. The drugstore is (behind / on) Maple Street.
3. The bus stop is (across from / in front of) the department store.
4. The movie theater is (next to / between) the department store.
5. The parking lot is (on / behind) the bank.
6. The school is (across from / next to) the park.

Around Town 25

Lesson 15 At the mall

1 Match the words to make the names of the places. Then write the names of the places.

1. movie __c__   a. rink   _movie theater_
2. bowling ____   b. arcade   _____
3. skating ____   c. theater   _____
4. candy ____   d. alley   _____
5. subway ____   e. store   _____
6. video ____   f. station   _____

2 Write questions and answers.

① Hitomi / bus stop

Q: _Is Hitomi at the bus stop?_
A: _No, she's not. She's at the skating rink._

② Eric and Kelly / Internet café

Q: _____
A: _____

③ Kevin / candy store

Q: _____
A: _____

④ Emily and Maria / video arcade

Q: _____
A: _____

⑤ Julia / skating rink

Q: _____
A: _____

⑥ Pedro / bookstore

Q: _____
A: _____

Lesson 16 — Any suggestions?

1 Look at the pictures. Write sentences using *bored, hot, hungry, thirsty,* or *tired*. Then write a suggestion from the box under each picture.

1. I'm bored.
2. _____

- ☐ Go swimming.
- ☐ Have a sandwich.
- ☐ Have a soda.
- ☑ Play volleyball.
- ☐ Sit down.

Play volleyball.

3. _____
4. _____
5. _____

2 Number the sentences in the correct order.

___ Bored? Well, go swimming or play volleyball.

_1_ Hello, Jim. How are you?

___ But I'm tired, too. I'm tired and bored.

___ Oh, hi, Lisa. I'm bored.

___ OK. Go to a movie. There's a good movie at the new movie theater.

___ Good idea. Let's go together.

Around Town 27

UNIT 4 Get Connected

1 Read the blog quickly. Write the ages.

Bored Betty _____   Weather William _____

---

www.SusanasSuggestions.gc

Ask Susana

👤 Hi, Susana!
I'm 13. My sister and I are bored. Any suggestions? We live in Smithtown.
– Bored Betty

👤 Hello, Bored Betty!
Go to Milton Mall. It's the biggest mall in your town. Look around the stores.
Go to Ricky's Restaurant. Have a sandwich and a soda. Go to a movie.
The movie theater is across from the mall. Have fun!
– Susana

👤 Good afternoon, Susana!
I'm 16. I'm at home with my dad. We're hot and we're bored.
Any suggestions? We live in Cedar Grove.
– Weather William

👤 Hello, Weather William!
Go to Weird Waterpark. It's on Main Street. It's behind the park.
Play on the waterslides. Go to Sammy's Sodas, and have a soda. Have fun!
– Susana

---

2 Complete the letters with the words in the box.

☐ across from ☐ biggest ☐ bored ✓ home ☐ waterslides

Hi, Susana!

I'm 14. I'm at _____home_____ , and I'm _____ . Any suggestions? I live in Lincoln.

– Helen at Home

Hello, Helen at Home!

Go to Freddy's Fun Park with some friends. It's the _____ amusement park there. It's _____ Village Mall. Play paintball or play on the _____ .
Enjoy!
– Susana

3 Read the blog in Part 1 slowly. Check (✓) Betty or William. Sometimes both are possible.

	Betty	William		Betty	William
1. Look around the stores.	✓		4. Go to Ricky's Restaurant.		
2. Go to a movie.			5. Have a soda.		
3. Play on the waterslides.			6. Have fun!		

UNIT 4 Check Yourself

1 Look at the map. Answer the questions with *Yes, it is,* or *No, it's not.*

1. Is the restaurant on Elm Street?
   Yes, it is.

2. Is the parking lot behind the movie theater?
   _____

3. Is the shoe store next to the café?
   _____

4. Is the bank across from the drugstore?
   _____

5. Is the bus stop in front of the bank?
   _____

2 Complete the questions with *Are* or *Is*. Then match the questions to the answers.

1. _Are_ you at home? _d_
2. _____ the park near the school? _____
3. _____ Ben and Jill here? _____
4. _____ you hot? _____
5. _____ the bank on Main Street? _____
6. _____ James at home? _____

a. No, they're not. They're late.
b. No, it's not. It's on State Street.
c. No, he's not. He's at the movie theater.
d. Yes, I am. I'm in my bedroom.
e. Yes, I am. Let's go swimming.
f. Yes, it is. It's next to the school.

3 Complete the conversations with the sentences in the box.

☑ I'm bored.   ☐ I'm hot.   ☐ I'm hungry.   ☐ I'm thirsty.   ☐ I'm tired.

1. A I'm bored.
   B Me, too. Let's play basketball.

2. A _____
   B Have a soda.

3. A _____
   B Let's sit down.

4. A _____
   B Have a sandwich.

5. A _____
   B Me, too. Let's go swimming.

Lesson 17 — My family

1 Look at the picture. Complete the sentences.

- Jorge, 65 — Rebecca, 63
- Julio, 44 — Laura, 42 — Leo, 32 — Rita, 30
- Carlos, 10 — Linda, 12 — Alicia, 8 — Ana, 2

1. Carlos is Linda's _brother_. He's _ten_.
2. Leo is Linda's _____. He's _____.
3. Rebecca is Linda's _____. She's _____.
4. Julio is Linda's _____. He's _____.
5. Alicia is Linda's _____. She's _____.
6. Laura is Linda's _____. She's _____.
7. Ana is Linda's _____. She's _____.
8. Rita is Linda's _____. She's _____.
9. Jorge is Linda's _____. He's _____.

2 Write sentences about Linda's family. Use *have* or *has*.

1. Linda's parents / three children
   Linda's parents have three children.
2. Carlos / two sisters
3. Linda, Carlos, and Alicia / one cousin
4. Laura / one brother
5. Linda / one aunt and one uncle
6. Carlos / no brothers
7. Alicia / one aunt
8. Leo / one sister
9. Linda / one sister and one brother
10. Ana / no sisters or brothers

UNIT 5 Family and Home

Lesson 18 — Family reunion

1 Complete the sentences with the words in the boxes.

1. ☐ smart   ☐ tall

   My cousin is not short. She's _____tall_____.
   My brother is _____smart_____. He likes math and science.

2. ☐ handsome   ☐ pretty

   My father is _____.
   My Aunt Linda is _____.

3. ☐ friendly   ☐ shy

   My best friend isn't shy. She's _____.
   My sister is not crazy. She's very _____.

2 Number the sentences in the correct order.

___ Mike? He's friendly and very funny.
___ She's smart. She's shy, too.
_1_ What's her name?
___ And your brother? What's he like?
___ Her name is Kayla. She's my sister.
___ What's she like?
___ Well, you're friendly and funny, too!

3 Answer the questions with your own information.

1. What's your best friend like?
   _____

2. What's your favorite actor like?
   _____

3. What's your math teacher like?
   _____

4. What's your favorite relative like?
   _____

5. What are you like?
   _____

Family and Home

Lessons 17 & 18 Mini-review

1 Check (✓) the word that is different.

1. ☐ thirty
   ☐ twenty-three
   ☑ friendly

2. ☐ uncle
   ☐ friend
   ☐ sister

3. ☐ hungry
   ☐ handsome
   ☐ pretty

4. ☐ friendly
   ☐ funny
   ☐ cousin

5. ☐ teacher
   ☐ father
   ☐ mother

6. ☐ sixty
   ☐ thin
   ☐ crazy

2 Look at the picture. Write *True* or *False*. Then correct the false statements.

Leonardo, 56 — Maria, 53

Gabriela, 23 — Michelle, 19 — Sergio, 17 — Joey, 11

1. Joey's mother is 23. _False. Joey's sister is 23._
2. His father is 56. _____
3. He has three brothers. _____
4. He has two sisters. _____
5. His brother is 10. _____

3 Laura is talking to Nick. Complete her sentences with *have*, *has*, or *'s*.

My name _'s_ Laura. I _____ one brother. He _____ eight, and his name _____ Vincent. He _____ really funny. I _____ a best friend. Her name _____ Julie. Julie _____ a little sister. She _____ only three. Her name _____ Kristen, and she _____ very pretty. Julie _____ a brother, too. He _____ handsome.

32 Unit 5

Lesson 19 — My new city

1 Match the words to the correct pictures.

1. happy _c_
2. old ___
3. sad ___
4. new ___
5. big ___
6. quiet ___

2 Complete the sentences with the words in Part 1.

1. Their neighborhood is noisy. It's not ___quiet___ .
2. Their school is old. It's not _____ .
3. We're sad. We're not _____ .
4. Our house is small. It's not _____ .

3 Combine the sentences. Use they're, we're, their, or our.

1. You're happy. I'm happy, too.
   We're happy.

2. Her neighborhood is quiet. His neighborhood is quiet, too.
   _____

3. He's from Canada. She's from Canada, too.
   _____

4. I'm a little sad. You're a little sad, too.
   _____

5. My school is new. Your school is new, too.
   _____

4 Circle the correct words to complete the sentences.

1. (They're / (Their)) school is very nice.
2. We miss Taro, but (our / we're) happy for him.
3. (They're / Our) soccer team is great this year.
4. (Their / We're) last name is Robbins.
5. (They're / Their) from Brazil.
6. (They're / Our) friends are funny.
7. (They're / Their) house isn't big.
8. (We're / Our) teacher is nice.
9. (They're / Their) not from Mexico.
10. (We're / Our) not thirsty.

Family and Home 33

Lesson 20 At home

1 Match the words in the box to the rooms in the house. Write the numbers.

> ❶ bathroom ❸ dining room ❺ kitchen ❼ yard
> ❷ bedroom   ❹ garage   ❻ living room

2 Complete the paragraph about the house in Part 1. Use *it's* or *it has*.

This is a new house. ___It's___ big. _____ in the city, so _____ a small yard. _____ four bedrooms and two bathrooms. _____ a nice kitchen and a big dining room. _____ a living room, too. _____ small, but pretty. _____ a garage. The neighborhood is nice. _____ quiet.

3 Circle the words that make the sentences true for you.

1. My home is in the (city / country).
2. It's (old / new).
3. Our neighborhood is (quiet / noisy).
4. Our (house / apartment) has a (big / small) kitchen.
5. It has (one / two / three / four / five) bedrooms.

UNIT 5 Get Connected

1 Read the article quickly. What's the name of Dave and Carol's house?

_____

Different Houses

A house in a tree!

Greg Sawyer is 12, and his sister, Jessica, is 8. They're children, but they have a house. It's a tree house! It's in the country. It's at their grandparents' house in Kansas. Their tree house has one room. It's a living room with a desk and a few chairs. It's small, but Greg and Jessica think it's great. Greg says, "I'm lucky. My tree house is really awesome!"

A house? A boat? A houseboat!

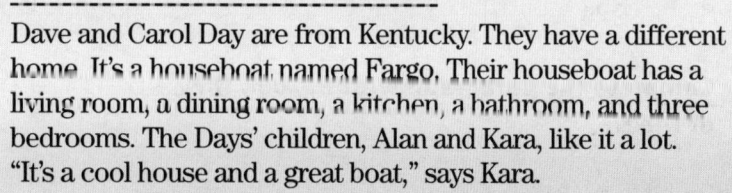

Dave and Carol Day are from Kentucky. They have a different home. It's a houseboat named Fargo. Their houseboat has a living room, a dining room, a kitchen, a bathroom, and three bedrooms. The Days' children, Alan and Kara, like it a lot. "It's a cool house and a great boat," says Kara.

2 Complete the sentences with the words in the box.

☐ awesome ☐ boat ☐ different ✓ lucky

1. My neighborhood has a big mall. I'm really ___lucky___ .
2. We're in _____ math classes. We're not in the same math class.
3. She thinks Zac Efron is _____ . He's her favorite star.
4. His house is in the water. He lives on a _____ .

3 Read the article in Part 1 slowly. Are these sentences true or false? Check (✓) True or False.

	True	False
1. Greg is 12.	☐	☐
2. Greg has two sisters.	☐	☐
3. The tree house is big.	☐	☐
4. The Days' houseboat has seven rooms.	☐	☐
5. The Days' houseboat is not cool.	☐	☐

Family and Home

UNIT 5 Check Yourself

1 Answer the questions. Use *it's, he's, she's, they're,* or *I'm* and the words in the box.

☐ big ☐ happy ☐ old ☐ quiet ☑ tall

1. **A** What's your aunt like? Is she short?
   B No, *she's not. She's tall.*

2. **A** What's your school like? Is it small?
   B No, _____

3. **A** What's your brother like? Is he noisy?
   B No, _____

4. **A** What are your CDs like? Are they new?
   B No, _____

5. **A** Are you sad today?
   B No, _____

2 Complete the paragraph with *we, our, they,* or *their*.

My family and our neighbors are different. _Our_ house is old, and _____ house is new. _____ have a big yard, and _____ have a small yard. But we like _____ house. _____ like their house, too.

3 Complete the sentences. Use *has* or *has no*.

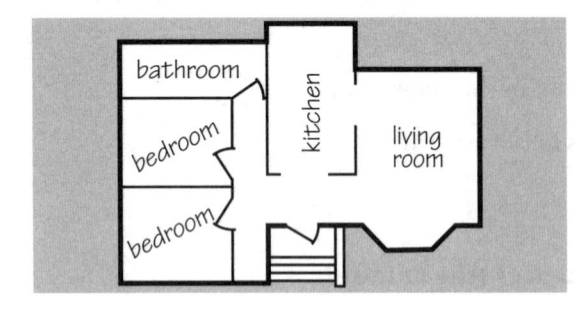

Jane's house

1. _It has two_ bedrooms.
2. _____ dining room.
3. _____ living room.

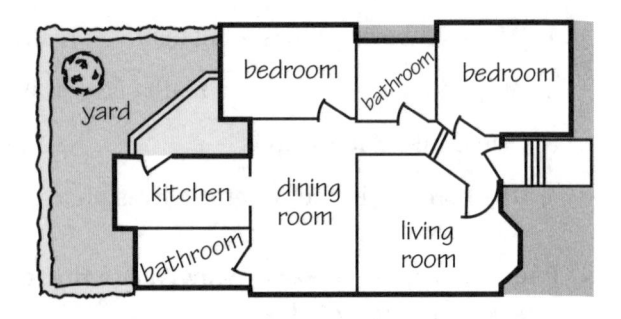

Tim's house

1. _____ yard.
2. _____ bathrooms.
3. _____ garage.

36 Check Yourself

Lesson 21 — The media center

1 Complete the crossword puzzle.

Across

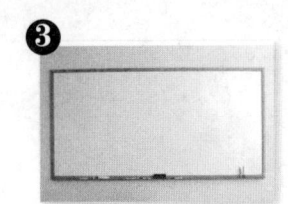

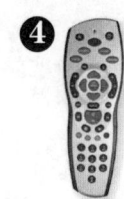

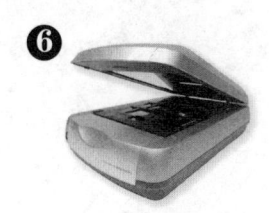

❸ ❹ ❻

Down

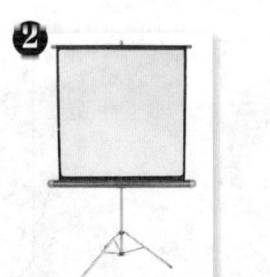

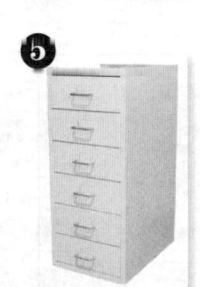

❶ ❸ ❷ ❺

(3 Across: B O A R D)

2 Complete the sentences with *there's a*, *there's no*, *there are*, or *there are no*.

1. _There are_ two printers.
2. _____ bookcase.
3. _____ board.
4. _____ screens.
5. _____ scanner.
6. _____ CD/DVD player.
7. _____ remote control.
8. _____ cabinets.

UNIT 6 At School

At School 37

Lesson 22: Around school

1 Complete the chart with the words in the box.

- ☑ auditorium ☐ cafeteria ☐ football field ☐ library ☐ swimming pool
- ☐ baseball field ☐ computer lab ☐ language lab ☐ soccer field ☐ tennis court

Sports facilities	School facilities
	auditorium

2 Circle the correct words to complete the conversation.

Angelo Rey, your school is cool. (**Is**/ Are) there a gym?

Rey Yes, there (is / are). There (is / are) three athletic fields, too.

Angelo (Are / Is) there (a / any) good football players?

Rey No, there (are / aren't). There (is / are) some good baseball players.

Angelo Is there (a / any) swimming pool?

Rey No, there (is / isn't). But there is a cafeteria. It's great!

Angelo Good. I'm hungry. Let's have a sandwich!

3 Complete the questions with *Is there a* or *Are there any*. Then answer the questions with your own information.

1. _Is there a_ swimming pool at your house?
   _____

2. _____ media center at your school?
   _____

3. _____ athletic fields in your neighborhood?
   _____

4. _____ tennis courts on your street?
   _____

5. _____ cafeteria at your school?
   _____

Lessons 20 & 21 Mini-review

1 Match the words to make the names of places and things. Then write the names of the places and things.

1. CD/DVD _f_   a. lab   _CD/DVD player_
2. computer ___   b. court   _____
3. tennis ___   c. field   _____
4. athletic ___   d. center   _____
5. remote ___   e. control   _____
6. media ___   f. player   _____

2 Complete the conversations.

1. **A** Are the facilities in your school nice? (Yes)
   B _Yes, they are._ We have great facilities!

2. **A** Are there any tennis courts at your school? (No)
   B _____ But we have three soccer fields.

3. **A** Is there a gym in your school? (Yes)
   B _____ It's next to the library.

4. **A** Are there any new students in your class? (Yes)
   B _____ They're from Puerto Rico.

5. **A** Is there a media center in your school? (No)
   B _____ But there's a new computer lab.

6. **A** Are there any good soccer players in your school? (Yes)
   B _____ Their names are Emily and Hugo.

7. **A** Is there a CD/DVD player in your classroom? (No)
   B _____ But there's a CD/DVD player in the media center.

8. **A** Is there a park near your school? (No)
   B _____ But there's a swimming pool.

3 Answer the questions in Part 2 with your own information.

1. _____   5. _____
2. _____   6. _____
3. _____   7. _____
4. _____   8. _____

At School 39

Lesson 23 — School subjects

1 Label the pictures with the words in the box.

☑ geography ☐ health ☐ history ☐ math ☐ music ☐ science

1. _geography_
2. _____
3. _____
4. _____
5. _____
6. _____

2 Complete the paragraph with *on* or *at*.

My school schedule is crazy! I have science __at__ 8:30 _____ Monday, Wednesday, and Friday. I think science is easy. I have math _____ 10:00 every day. Math is difficult. I have music _____ Tuesday and Thursday _____ 11:00. It's fun. I have computer lab _____ Monday and Wednesday _____ 1:00. It's my favorite class. I don't like history. I have history every day _____ 2:00.

3 Are these statements true or false for you? Write *True* or *False*. Then correct the false statements.

1. I have six classes every day.

2. History is my favorite class.

3. I have English on Monday.

4. Art is difficult.

5. I think science is easy.

6. I have math at 10:45 on Monday.

Lesson 24 — Spring Day

1 Match the two ways to say the same time.

1. It's eight forty-five. _c_
2. It's two fifty. ___
3. It's seven fifteen. ___
4. It's three twenty-five. ___
5. It's twelve forty. ___
6. It's eleven fifty-five ___

a. It's twenty-five after three.
b. It's ten to three.
c. It's a quarter to nine.
d. It's twenty to one.
e. It's five to twelve.
f. It's a quarter after seven.

2 What time is it now? Write the answer two ways.

_____

_____

3 Look at the information on Jake's schedule. Write questions and answers.

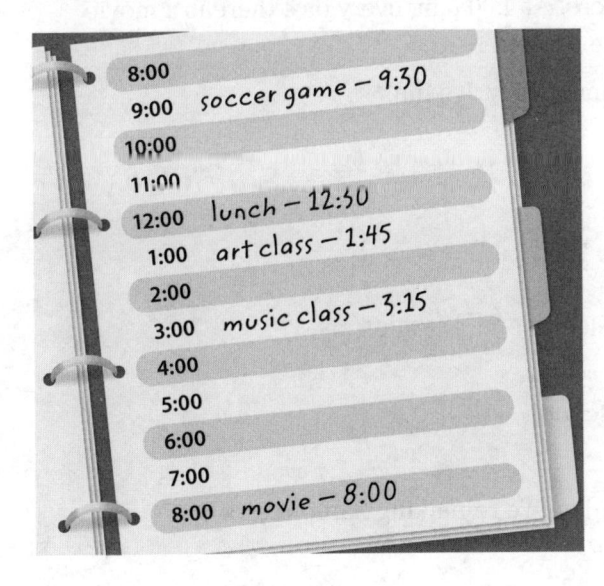

Schedule:
- 8:00
- 9:00 soccer game — 9:30
- 10:00
- 11:00
- 12:00 lunch — 12:50
- 1:00 art class — 1:45
- 2:00
- 3:00 music class — 3:15
- 4:00
- 5:00
- 6:00
- 7:00
- 8:00 movie — 8:00

1. Q: _What time is the soccer game?_
   A: It's at nine thirty.

2. Q: What time is the movie?
   A: _____

3. Q: _____
   A: It's at three fifteen.

4. Q: What time is lunch?
   A: _____

5. Q: What time is his art class?
   A: _____

4 What time is it now? Write the times.

1. _It's eleven o'clock._
2. _____
3. _____
4. _____
5. _____
6. _____

At School 41

UNIT 6 Get Connected

1 Read the Web site quickly. Underline the times.

www.campcrazy/summer.gc

Camp Crazy!

Welcome to Camp Crazy. It's a summer camp. There are cool classes every day. At 10:00 a.m., there are 3D animation classes, juggling classes, fashion design classes, and cooking classes. They're in the gym.

There are language classes in the media center at 11:00 a.m. Lunch is in the cafeteria at 12:00 p.m.

There are sports at 1:30 p.m. on the athletic fields and in the gym. There are soccer, baseball, and basketball team practices. At 4:00 p.m. every day, there is a movie in our movie theater.

Come to Camp Crazy. It's fun!

2 Complete the sentences with the words in the box.

☐ animation ☑ baseball ☐ cooking ☐ summer ☐ fashion

1. I'm on the ____baseball____ team at school.
2. This video game has really cool _____.
3. I have _____ class on Monday. We're making hamburgers.
4. We don't have school in _____.
5. That model knows a lot about _____.

3 Read the Web site in Part 1 slowly. Complete the schedule.

Time	Activity	Place
10:00 a.m.	3D animation, fashion design, and cooking	gym
	language class	media center
12:00 p.m.	lunch	
1:30 p.m.	sports	
	movie	movie theater

UNIT 6 Check Yourself

1 Look at the picture. Write questions and answers.

1. (CDs) Q: _Are there any CDs?_ A: _Yes, there are._
2. (CD/DVD player) Q: _____ A: _____
3. (computers) Q: _____ A: _____
4. (printers) Q: _____ A: _____
5. (remote control) Q: _____ A: _____
6. (bookcase) Q: _____ A: _____

2 Look at the picture. Write sentences with *There's a*, *There's no*, *There are*, or *There are no*.

1. (bookcase) _There's no bookcase._
2. (cabinets) _____
3. (screen) _____
4. (books) _____
5. (chairs) _____
6. (printer) _____

3 Write sentences about Gary's schedule.

1. _His English class is at 1:30._
2. _____
3. _____
4. _____
5. _____
6. _____

GARY'S SCHEDULE

Event
1. English class 1:30
2. history class 8:15
3. music class Friday
4. health class Wednesday
5. geography class 10:35
6. science class 11:45

Check Yourself 43

Lesson 25 — People and countries

1 Complete the puzzle with seven countries. What's the mystery word?

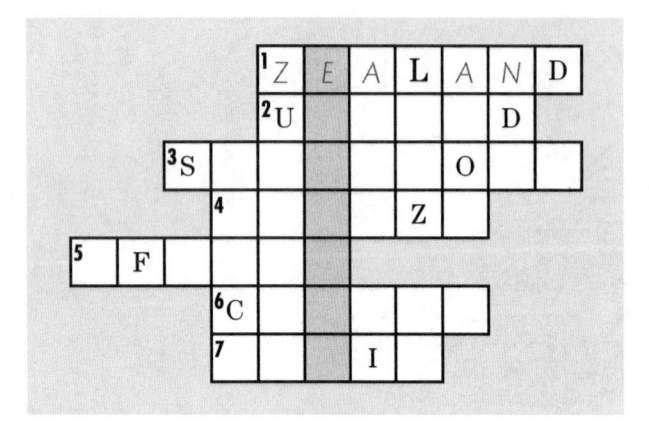

```
1 Z E A L A N D
  2 U     D
3 S     O
    4   Z
5 F
  6 C
  7     I
```

1. New _____ is near Australia.
2. Baseball is popular in the _____ States.
3. In _____, people speak English and Chinese.
4. _____ is small and interesting.
5. People in South _____ speak English, but not American English.
6. The United States is between _____ and Mexico.
7. Delhi is very big city in _____.

2 Circle the correct words to complete the conversation.

Carla You have a lot of friends, José. Are they from Belize?

José No, they (are / (aren't)). They're from England.

Carla And this girl? (Is / Are) she from England?

José Yes, she (is / isn't). She's great.

Carla This boy is cute. (Is / Are) he from England, too?

José No, he (aren't / isn't). (He's / She's) from Canada. He has six sisters.

Carla Wow!

3 Complete the questions with *Is* or *Are*. Then answer the questions with your own information.

1. _____ your city or town in the U.S.? _____
2. _____ you from South Africa? _____
3. _____ your teachers from England? _____
4. _____ your best friend from India? _____

Lesson 26: Nationalities

1 Write the sentences another way.

1. Susana is from Brazil.
   She's Brazilian.

2. Teresa is from Mexico.

3. Mike and Tommy are from Australia.

4. Keiko is from Japan.

5. James is from England.

6. Ben and Katy are from the United States.

2 Are these statements true or false for you? Check (✓) True or False. Then correct the false statements.

	True	False
1. My first language is English.	☐	✓

My first language isn't English. It's Spanish.

2. My parents are from Spain. ☐ ☐

3. My English teacher is Canadian. ☐ ☐

4. My favorite cartoon character is Japanese. ☐ ☐

5. My favorite actor is from Puerto Rico. ☐ ☐

6. My best friend is from Singapore. ☐ ☐

Around the World 45

Lessons 25 & 26 Mini-review

1 Check (✓) the word that is different.

1. ☐ Peruvian
   ☐ French
   ☑ Japan

2. ☐ England
   ☐ Rio de Janeiro
   ☐ Peru

3. ☐ Australia
   ☐ South Korean
   ☐ Brazil

4. ☐ Japanese
   ☐ Spain
   ☐ Mexican

5. ☐ Brazilian
   ☐ Canada
   ☐ the United States

6. ☐ New Zealand
   ☐ Indian
   ☐ Singapore

2 Complete the paragraph with *is*, *isn't*, *are*, and *aren't*.

My favorite actor __is__ Hugh Jackman. Hugh _____ from Australia. He _____ American, but he _____ a big star in the United States. His movies _____ sad and quiet. They _____ usually action movies. He _____ a very good singer. His musicals _____ very nice. His romantic movies _____ also nice and funny. He _____ really cute.

3 Check (✓) the correct responses.

1. Is he from Vancouver?
   ☐ No, they aren't.
   ☑ Yes, he is.

2. Is Russell Crowe Canadian?
   ☐ Yes, it is.
   ☐ No, he isn't. He's Australian.

3. Are they from France?
   ☐ Yes, they are.
   ☐ Yes, she is.

4. Is she from Japan?
   ☐ No, he isn't. He's from South Korea.
   ☐ Yes, she is. She's a famous singer.

5. Are Marco and Sergio from South Africa?
   ☐ No, they aren't. They're from Brazil.
   ☐ Yes, they are great baseball players.

6. Is Gil de Ferran Brazilian?
   ☐ Yes, he is. He's great.
   ☐ Yes, they are. They're interesting.

Lesson 27 — Holidays

1 Circle the correct words to make the sentences true for the United States.

1. Thanksgiving is in (July / (November) / December).
2. Valentine's Day is in (March / May / February).
3. New Year's Eve is in (December / January / February).
4. Independence Day is in (July / June / January).

2 Write the missing months. Complete the series.

1. September   October   _November_   _____
2. March   _____ May   _____
3. _____   February   _____   April
4. June   _____ August   _____
5. _____   March   April   _____
6. _____   _____ December

3 Complete the conversations with the sentences in the box.

- ☐ It's in February.
- ☐ It's in May.
- ☐ It's in October. It's a fun holiday.
- ☑ It's July. My favorite holiday is Independence Day.
- ☐ It's New Year's Eve. It's in December.
- ☐ Yes, it is. It's great.

1. **A** What's your favorite month?
   B _It's July. My favorite holiday is Independence Day._

2. **A** When is Valentine's Day in the U.S.?
   B _____

3. **A** When is Thanksgiving in Canada?
   B _____

4. **A** When is Mother's Day?
   B _____

5. **A** What's your favorite holiday?
   B _____

6. **A** Is Children's Day your favorite holiday?
   B _____

Around the World 47

Lesson 28: Important days

1 Complete the crossword puzzle with words for these numbers.

Across
5. 18th
6. 24th
8. 1st
9. 3rd
10. 30th

Down
1. 6th
2. 17th
3. 10th
4. 13th
7. 5th

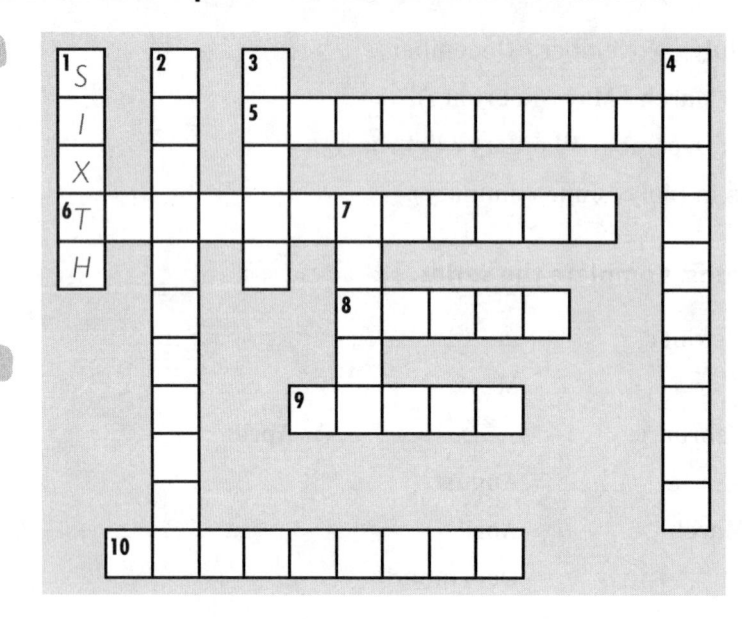

2 Complete the paragraph with *in* or *on*.

Valentine's Day is ___on___ February 14th, Thanksgiving is _____ November, and Christmas is _____ December 25th. But what about Video Game Day? It's _____ September 12th. And Thank You Day? It's _____ September 18th. Here are some good holidays for the family: Sisters' Day is _____ August 4th, Aunts' and Uncles' Day is _____ July 16th, and Family Week is _____ May. But my favorite holiday is _____ September. It's _____ September 4th – that's Teacher's Day!

3 Complete the sentences with *in* or *on* and your own information.

1. My first day of school is _____.
2. My birthday is _____.
3. I'm always happy _____.
4. There are a lot of holidays _____.

48 Unit 7

UNIT 7 Get Connected

1 Read the article quickly. When is Valentine's Day in Brazil?

_____

♥ Valentine's Day Around the World ♥

Valentine's Day is on February 14th in many countries – the United States, Canada, India, England, and Peru. In Peru, the name for Valentine's Day is the Day of Love and Friendship. In Brazil, Valentine's Day is on June 12th.

On Valentine's Day in the United States, many boys give girls flowers. In South Korea and Japan on this day, girls give boys chocolate or candy. Then on March 14th – on White Day – boys give girls chocolate or candy.

When is Valentine's Day in your country? Is it a fun holiday?

2 Choose the correct word to complete the sentences.

1. Let's have a (celebration / holiday) for my birthday.
2. It's an (important / August) holiday in the U.S., Mexico, and other countries.
3. People (receive / chocolate) gifts on their birthdays.
4. New Year's Eve is a big (month / holiday) in many countries.

3 Read the article in Part 1 slowly. Then answer the questions.

1. Is Valentine's Day on February 14th in Canada? _Yes, it is._
2. Is The Day of Love and Friendship a celebration in the U.S.? _____
3. Is Valentine's Day on June 12th in Peru? _____
4. Is White Day a celebration in Japan and South Korea? _____

Around the World 49

UNIT 7 Check Yourself

1 Complete the conversation with *is, isn't, are,* or *aren't.*

Lee Hey, Deb. Look at all of my CDs.

Deb Wow! You have a lot of CDs.

Lee Yes, and this _____ my favorite CD. This _____ Luciana Mello. She's my favorite singer.

Deb _____ she famous?

Lee No, she _____ . But she's great.

Deb _____ all your favorite singers Brazilian?

Lee No, they _____ . I like American singers, too.

2 Write questions.

1. A (England) *Is he from England?*
   B Yes, he is. He's British.

2. A (Peruvian) _____
   B No, they aren't. Tia and Marie are Colombian.

3. A (April) _____
   B No, it isn't. Mother's Day is in May.

4. A (good) _____
   B Yes, they are. The Orioles are a good baseball team!

5. A (Brazil) _____
   B No, he isn't. He's from Puerto Rico.

3 Write sentences about people's birthdays.

	Month	Day
1. Sebastian	9	5
2. Shannon	2	
3. Mr. Brock	12	21
4. Paco	4	11
5. Kelly	8	

1. *Sebastian's birthday is on September 5th.*
2. *Shannon's birthday is in . . .*
3. _____
4. _____
5. _____

4 Write the words.

1. 14th *fourteenth*
2. 4th _____
3. 23rd _____
4. 9th _____
5. 16th _____
6. 22nd _____

50 Check Yourself

Lesson 29: Favorite places

1 Circle the correct words to complete the sentences.

1. My favorite store is Hip-Hop Clothes. There are cool clothes in the store, and it's always (**busy** / quiet).
2. There are a lot of museums, parks, and restaurants in London. It's (cute / exciting). It isn't (boring / happy).
3. The beach is my favorite place for a vacation. There aren't a lot of stores at the beach, and it's (beautiful / noisy).
4. The city zoo has lots of animals. It's (fun / old), and the animals are cute.
5. The Getty Museum in Los Angeles isn't (boring / crazy). You can learn a lot there. It's very (small / interesting).

2 Complete the conversation with the sentences in the box.

- ☐ It's really interesting.
- ☐ It's the Kennedy Space Center.
- ☐ What's it like?
- ☐ What's your favorite place in Florida, Steve?
- ☑ What's your favorite place in Florida, Talisa?

Steve _What's your favorite place in Florida, Talisa?_

Talisa It's the city of Naples.

Steve _____

Talisa It's exciting. There are a lot of fun things there. There are beautiful beaches, stores, museums, and parks.

Steve Wow! That's great.

Talisa _____

Steve _____

Talisa What's it like?

Steve _____

Lesson 30 — Talent show

1 Write the words in the correct column.

☑ dance ☐ draw ☐ Ping-Pong ☐ sing ☐ skateboard ☐ the guitar

I can . . .	I can play . . .
dance,	

2 Number the sentences in the correct order.

___ Great! I can sing. Let's enter.
___ Can Mary sing?
___ No. I can't dance at all. But I can play the guitar.
___ You and me? Good idea!
_1_ It's a talent show. Hey! There's Mary's name.
___ No, she can't. But she can dance.
___ Can you dance?

3 Look at the pictures. Write questions and answers.

❶
Q: Can he sing?
A: No, he can't.

❷
Q: _____
A: _____

❸
Q: _____
A: _____

❹
Q: _____
A: _____

4 Write sentences about yourself. Use *I can* and *I can't*.

1. _____
2. _____
3. _____
4. _____

Lessons 29 & 30 Mini-review

1 Answer the questions with the information in the chart.

	Ethan	Brenda
sing	☐	✓
draw	✓	✓
play the guitar	✓	☐
dance	☐	✓

1. Can Brenda play the guitar? _No, she can't._
2. Can Ethan draw? _____
3. Can Brenda dance? _____
4. Can Ethan sing? _____
5. Can Brenda draw? _____
6. Can Ethan dance? _____

2 Complete the questions with *What's* or *Can*. Then answer the questions.

1. _What's_ your English class like?
   _____
2. _____ your math class like?
   _____
3. _____ your best friend skateboard?
   _____
4. _____ your favorite city like?
   _____
5. _____ you speak Spanish?
   _____
6. _____ your teacher play the guitar?
   _____

3 Complete conversation 1. Then complete conversation 2 with your own information.

1. **A** What's your favorite place in Puerto Rico?
   B _It's Old San Juan._ (Old San Juan)
   A What's it like?
   B _____ (beautiful / interesting)

2. **A** _____ in your town?
   B _____
   A What's it like?
   B _____

Teen Time 53

Lesson 31 — School fashion

1 Label the clothes with the words in the box.

1 blouse	☐ pants	☐ shoes	☐ skirt	☐ socks	☐ tie
☐ jacket	☐ shirt	☐ shorts	☐ sneakers	☐ sweater	☐ T-shirt

TARA TAKESHI MARK

2 Write questions.

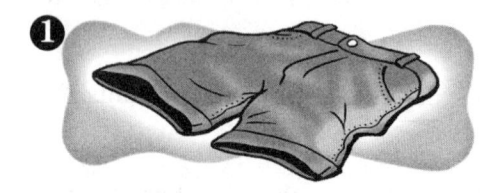

❶ *What color are the shorts?*

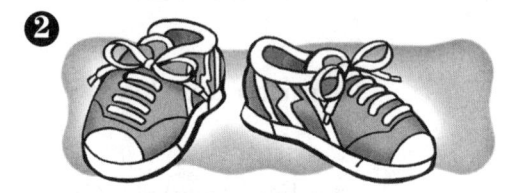

They're blue.

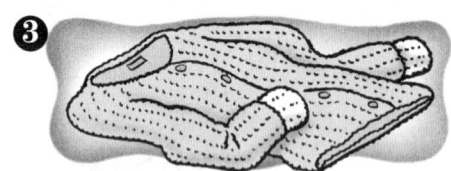

❷ _____

They're green and white.

❸ _____

It's green.

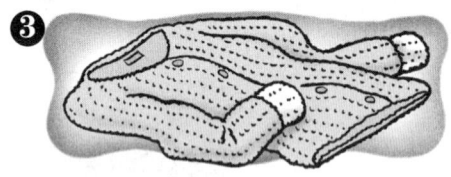

❹ _____

They're brown.

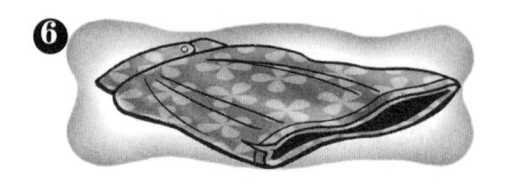

❺ _____

It's blue and red.

❻ _____

It's pink and purple.

54   Unit 8

Lesson 32 — Teen tastes

1 Write each conversation in the correct order.

1. ☐ Oh, I don't like rap music. I like pop music.
   ☐ It's my new rap CD. My favorite music is rap.
   ☑ What's this?

   A *What's this?*
   B _____
   A _____

2. ☐ I like pop music, too. But my favorite music is classical.
   ☐ I like pop music. What about you, Amy?
   ☐ That's great! I like classical music, too.

   A _____
   B _____
   A _____

2 Are these statements true or false for you? Check (✓) True or False. Then correct the false statements.

	True	False
1. I don't like comic books. I think they're boring.	☐	☑
I love comic books. They're cool.		
2. I love classical music. It's beautiful.	☐	☐
3. I don't like basketball. I think it's difficult.	☐	☐
4. I like science. It's easy for me.	☐	☐
5. I don't like music stores. They're too noisy!	☐	☐

Teen Time 55

UNIT 8 Get Connected

1 Read the Web site quickly. When is the city fair?

_____

www.cityfair/oakdale.gc

A CITY CELEBRATION

Come to Oakdale's City <u>Fair</u> on June 14th. It's a big party. The fair is <u>cheap</u>. A ticket is only five dollars. There are some really nice things at the fair.

- There's great music.
  You can listen to <u>jazz</u> and rap.
  You can <u>sing</u> and dance, too.
- There's great food. You can eat Korean, <u>Peruvian</u>, and Chinese food.
- There's <u>shopping</u> at the fair.
  You can buy T-shirts, CDs, backpacks, and hats.
- There are games at the fair, too!

Please come. It's always fun.

2 Complete the paragraph with the underlined words from Part 1.

This street ___*fair*___ is awesome. You can listen to _____. You can _____ songs, too. You can even eat _____ food! The _____ is great. The T-shirts are only six dollars! They're _____.

3 Read the Web site in Part 1 slowly. Write *True* or *False*. Then correct the false statements.

1. The city fair is in Pineville. _False. It's in Oakdale._
2. The fair is in October. _____
3. The city fair is a big party. _____
4. The fair is cheap. _____
5. There's rock music at the fair. _____
6. You can play games at the fair. _____

UNIT 8 Check Yourself

1 Complete the conversations with the questions in the box.

☐ What color are your shoes? ☐ What's the zoo like?
☐ What color is your cell phone? ☑ What's your school like?

1. A *What's your school like?*
   B It's busy. It has a lot of students.

2. A _____
   B It's pink. It's really cute!

3. A _____
   B It's interesting. There are a lot of animals.

4. A _____
   B They're blue. They're old, too.

2 Match the questions to the answers.

1. What's your favorite food? *e*
2. What's your favorite school subject? ___
3. What's your math class like? ___
4. What's the museum like? ___
5. What's your favorite music? ___
6. What's your soccer coach like? ___

a. Rap. It's really cool!
b. She's nice. And she can play very well!
c. It's boring. I don't like math.
d. I like science. It's fun.
e. Italian. I love pizza!
f. It's busy, but very interesting.

3 Complete the paragraph with *can*, *can't*, *like*, *love*, or *don't like*.

My favorite place in Sydney is Bondi Beach. It's very exciting and interesting. I *don't like* boring places. I _____ the water and the sun. I _____ swim very well, too. My brother _____ swim. But he _____ skateboard! So Bondi Beach is his favorite place, too.

Check Yourself 57

Illustration Credits

Adolar Mendes 22, 37, 40, 41, 43, 50
Michael Brennan 6, 20 *(top)*, 23, 34, 43 *(bottom)*
Andrea Champlin 16, 24
Laurie Conley 7, 13, 18 *(bottom)*, 19 *(top)*, 27, 48
David Coulson 12, 22, 26
Bruce Day 2, 29 *(bottom)*, 44, 48
Adam Hurwitz 36 *(bottom)*
Larry Jones 3, 8, 36 *(top)*, 39, 52, 54
Marcelo Pacheco 7, 17, 20 *(bottom)*, 21, 27, 32, 55
Félix Reiners 5, 9, 18, 19, 30, 31
Andrew Schiff 25, 29 *(top)*
Sattu Rodrigues 19

Photo Acknowledgements

The authors and publishers acknowledge the following sources of copyright material and are grateful for the permissions granted. While every effort has been made, it has not always been possible to identify the sources of all the material used, or to trace all copyright holders. If any omissions are brought to our notice, we will be happy to include the appropriate acknowledgements on reprinting.

Workbook

p.2: ©Peter Griffith/Masterfile; p.3 (1): ©Steve Prezant/Masterfile; p.3 (2): ©Blend Images/Shutterstock; p.3 (3): ©RAW FILE/Masterfile; p. 3 (4): ©Jack Wild/Taxi Japan/Getty Images; p.4 (T): ©Elizabeth Knox/Masterfile; p.4 (B): ©Keith Brofsky/UpperCut Images/Getty Images Plus/Getty Images; p.7 (small dog): ©Erik Lam/Shutterstock; p.7 (large dog): ©Artiga Photo/Corbis; p.7 (girl+dog): ©Stockbyte/Getty Images; p.10 (T): Steve Granitz/WireImage; p.10 (TC): ©Andrew Kent/Corbis; p.10 (C): ©Jim Spellman/WireImage/Getty Images; p.10 (BC): ©Shirlaine Forrest/Getty Images for MTV; p.10 (B): ©ILLUMINATION ENTERTAINMENT/THE KOBAL COLLECTION; p.11 (TL): ©David Young-Wolff/The Image Bank/Getty Images; p.11 (TR): ©Hilary Brodey/Photodisc/Getty Images; p.11 (BL): ©Albert L. Ortega/Getty Images; p.11 (BR): ©Jaroslaw Wojcik/Getty Images; P.13: ©Kali Nine LLC/iStock/Getty Images Plus; P.14 (L): © 2/Inti St. Clair/Ocean/Corbis; P.14 (R): ©Camille Tokerud/Photodisc/Getty Images; P.15 (1): ©SuperstudioThe Image Bank/Getty Images; P.15 (2): ©Mike Marsland/WireImage/Getty Images; P.15 (3): ©John Schults/ZUMA/Corbis; P.15 (4): ©DreamPictures/Blend Images/Getty Images; P.15 (5): ©Jesse D. Garrabrant/NBAE via Getty Images; P.15 (6): © l i g h t p o e t/Shutterstock; P.15 (7): ©ILLUMINATION ENTERTAINMENT/THE KOBAL COLLECTION; P.15 (8): ©Anton Oparin/Shutterstock; P.15 (Adventure Time): ©Cartoon Network/Everett/REX; p.15 (Nadal): ©DOMINIQUE FAGET/AFP/Getty Images; p.19 (1): ©Mindscape studio/Shutterstock; p.19 (2): ©Jeff Blackler/REX; p.19 (3): ©Hulton Archive/Getty Images; p.19 (4): ©COLUMBIA PICTURES / THE KOBAL COLLECTION; p.19 (5 red): ©GaryAlvis/E+/Getty Images; p.19 (5 blue): ©clu/iStock / Getty Images Plus/Getty Images; p.19 (6): ©Anthony Berenyi/Shutterstock; p.23: © KL Services/Masterfile/Corbis; p.27: ©Vikram Raghuvanshi/iStock / Getty Images Plus/Getty Images; p.28: ©Ariel Skelley/Blend Images/Getty Images; p.33 (a): ©Nathan Griffith/Alamy; p.33 (b): © Jose Luis Pelaez, Inc./Blend Images/Corbis; p.33 (c): ©SW Productions/Stockbyte/Getty Images; p.33 (d): ©Tom Le Goff/Photodisc/Getty Images; p.33 (e): ©Robert Churchill/E+/Getty Images; p.33 (f): ©Johan Swanepoel/Shutterstock; p.33 (C "busy"): © Sergiu Turcanu / Alamy; p.33 (B: "quiet"): © William Manning / Alamy; p.35 (T): ©Paul Bradforth/Alamy; p.35 (B): ©Scott Leigh/iStock/Getty Images Plus/Getty Images; p.37 (3): ©Meiko Arquillos/UpperCut Images/Getty Images; p.37 (4): ©© Finnbarr Webster/Alamy; p.37 (6): ©Hugh Threlfall/Alamy; p.37 (1): ©Dragan/Shutterstock; p.37 (2): ©Suzanne Tucker/Shutterstock; p.37 (3): ©Catapult/Getty Images; p.37 (5): ©Aaron Amat/Shutterstock; p.38 (T): David Schmidt/Masterfile; p.38 (B): © ClassicStock / Alamy; p.42: © Brian Mitchell/Corbis; p.45(1): Karin Dreyer/Blend Images/Getty Images; p.45(2): ©Denis Kuvaev/Shutterstock; p.45(3): ©Andreas Pollok/The Image Bank/Getty Images; p.45(4): ©DAJ/Getty Images; p.45(5): ©Michael Prince/Corbis; p.45(6): ©Toby Burrows/Photodisc/Getty Images; p.46 (L): ©Walter McBride/WireImage/Getty Images; p.46 (R): ©20TH CENTURY FOX / THE KOBAL COLLECTION / HAYES, KERRY; p.47: ©Ron Stroud/Masterfile; p.49: ©Datacraft Co Ltd; p.50: ©racorn/Shutterstock; p.51 (L): ©James Randklev/Photographer's Choice RF/Getty Images; p.51 (R): ©NASA - digital version copyright Science Faction/Getty Images; p.53 (TL): ©Jake Hellbach/Alamy; p.53 (TR): ©Jason Lugo/E+/Getty Images; p.53 (B): ©Richard Cummins/Robert Harding World Imagery/Getty Images; p.56: © Jeff Greenberg / Alamy; p.57 (T): © Monkey Business Images/Monkey Business/Corbis; p.57 (BL): ©Dave G. Houser/Corbis; p.57 (BL): ©Paul A. Souders/Corbis

Cover photograph by Joe McBride/Getty Images.

Notes

Notes